The Cognitive Layer

Human Cognition in the Age of Externalized Intelligence

Xiaoqing Wang

The Cognitive Layer

Human Cognition in the Age of Externalized Intelligence

First edition, 2026.

Interior design and text by Xiaoqing Wang.

Preface

A person returns to a long project after weeks away.

The files are still there. The folder opens. The notes have not disappeared. The old draft still contains its headings, comments, and unfinished sections. A repository still builds. A shared document still shows its revision history. Nothing obvious has been lost.

Yet the person cannot fully get back in.

The project has survived as material, but the path back into thought has weakened. The file records what was written. It does not always preserve why a passage was rejected, why one tone mattered, why a decision was postponed, or why an unresolved question had to remain open. The project is present, but its reasoning environment has cooled.

This book begins from that ordinary experience.

More human cognition now lives outside the individual mind. This is not entirely new. Writing, calendars, libraries, maps, diagrams, ledgers, archives, and institutions have long carried parts of memory and reasoning beyond the body. Serious thought has never been purely internal. It has always depended on supports that hold, stabilize, compare, and return.

What is changing is the density and responsiveness of those supports.

Notes, project archives, version control systems, shared documents, and AI tools do not merely store finished information. They increasingly preserve context, decision trails, failed paths, unfinished reasoning, working standards, and unresolved questions. They help a person or team return to long work after interruption. They can remember that a manuscript rejected a certain voice, that a codebase avoided a dependency for reasons of reversibility, or that a research inquiry left a category provisional because the evidence was not yet stable.

These systems do not think for us in the full human sense. They do not possess judgment, responsibility, or consequence. But they can carry enough of the surrounding structure of work to change how thought resumes. A person may no longer return only to a file. They may return to a remembered project environment.

That change is useful. It is also dangerous.

When continuity is preserved outside the mind, return becomes easier. The burden of re-explaining the project can fall. Work can survive interruption with less waste. A team can recover why earlier decisions were made. An institution can inspect how a policy or technical standard evolved.

But preserved context can also acquire authority it does not deserve. A memory can feel like judgment because it arrives fluently. A prior decision can feel settled because the system recalls it clearly. A project can become too loyal to its former self. A platform can become the only place where the work still makes sense.

The Cognitive Layer examines that pressure.

Several exclusions matter. This is not an AI productivity book or a guide to working faster, producing more, or organizing a better workflow. Productivity may be affected by the systems described here, but speed is not the central question.

It is not a book about artificial general intelligence, AI consciousness, or future machine minds. The argument concerns ordinary work already visible in manuscripts, codebases, research archives, institutions, and long collaborative projects. Continuity is not consciousness. Presence is not personhood.

Nor is it a prompt manual or an argument that machines replace human thought. The book does not teach the reader how to ask better questions of a model. It asks what happens when external systems support memory, comparison, synthesis, and continuity without absorbing human judgment.

This book is written for people who live inside long projects: writers, engineers, researchers, founders, teams, and institutions who feel the cost of lost context, stale memory, platform dependence, and decisions that become difficult to own.

The book is instead a serious nonfiction examination of memory, continuity, externalized cognition, cognitive archives, portability, judgment authority, and human agency. It asks what happens when tools begin to remember not only outputs, but parts of the reasoning environment around outputs. It asks how long work survives interruption. It asks what must remain inspectable when context is preserved by systems outside the person. It asks how decisions remain accountable when they are shaped by archives, models, and platforms.

Several distinctions guide the argument.

Memory is not judgment. A system may preserve a decision trail without knowing what should now be done.

Assistance is not authority. A model may help compare, draft, summarize, and retrieve. It does not own the consequence of action.

These distinctions are not defensive qualifications. They are the conditions under which externalized cognition can be used responsibly. If the systems described here are treated as minds, the analysis becomes inflated. If they are treated as mere storage, the analysis becomes too small.

The question is more difficult than either position allows.

External systems can now support cognition in ways that are persistent, responsive, and consequential. They can help carry context across interruption. They can make project history visible. They can reduce cognitive loss. They can also conceal stale assumptions, enclose continuity inside platforms, and make human approval thinner than human judgment.

The question is not whether external systems can support cognition. They already do.

The question is how human judgment remains accountable when they do.

Contents

Chapter 1

Tools That Remember

How ordinary tools become cognitive infrastructure when they retain context across time.

1.1 The Tool That Does Not Reset

A tool usually announces itself by what it lets a person do.

A hammer concentrates force. A wheel carries weight. A clock regularizes time. A spreadsheet holds calculations that would quickly exceed unaided attention. A search engine retrieves an answer that once might have required a library, a specialist, or a patient afternoon of looking.

Most tools, however powerful, have a simple temporal shape. The person approaches, uses the tool, and leaves. When the person returns, the tool is available again, but the relation has not moved forward. The saw does not remember the table. The clock does not remember the day it helped divide. The word processor preserves the file, but not the hesitation before the paragraph or the reason a sentence was removed.

This has been one of the quiet assumptions beneath modern software. Programs store files, preferences, window positions, histories, and cursor locations. They can reopen the last workspace. They can preserve the artifact. But the artifact is not the reasoning environment around the artifact.

The file survived. The reasoning environment did not.

AI changes this relation when it remembers enough of the project for the next interaction to begin from within the work rather than outside it. The change is often described as intelligence, automation, or speed. Those descriptions are not wrong, but they arrive too early. The deeper shift begins when the tool no longer fully resets.

A remembered tool is not a conscious tool. It is not a collaborator in the human sense. It is not an authority over the work. It is an interactive system that preserves enough prior context to alter the human act of return.

A writer comes back to a manuscript after several weeks. The folder opens. The draft opens. The notes remain. Yet the writer has to reconstruct why the introduction was being rewritten, why a warmer voice had been rejected, why a chapter needed to delay its conclusion, why the book had to distinguish continuity from consciousness. A remembered system can reduce that reconstruction. It may recall that the manuscript rejects hype, that one metaphor was too social, that a certain distinction must remain cold, that the next revision was supposed to clarify the boundary between memory and judgment.

Nothing in that scene requires a mind inside the machine. But the human does not return to a blank room.

Something of the working arrangement has survived.

1.2 When Return Changes the Tool

The practical effect first appears as convenience. Less repetition. Fewer reminders. Faster resumption. A user no longer has to restate every constraint before useful work can begin.

But convenience is only the surface. A remembered tool changes the temporal structure of work. It shortens the distance between arrival and participation. The user is not merely reopening a document or prompting a system. The user is re-entering a partly maintained field of orientation.

Older software often stored state without preserving meaning. A browser history records where one has been, not what one was trying to understand. A task manager carries an item forward, not the uncertainty that made the item difficult. A code repository records commits, but the reason a dependency was rejected may live only in a conversation, a meeting, or a developer's memory. A research folder may contain the paper that mattered while losing the tension that made it matter.

Remembered tools begin to hold some of those surrounding conditions. They can preserve an old refusal, a standard formed during revision, a list of paths already examined, a working vocabulary, an unresolved question. They do not preserve the whole living pressure of the work. They preserve enough to matter.

This is why the change should not be reduced to storage. Storage keeps material available. Remembered interaction keeps parts of the work's orientation active. A manuscript system may remember that the chapter should not become prompt-engineering advice. A code assistant may remember that reversibility matters more than a fashionable dependency. A research assistant may remember that a category remains provisional because later evidence may collapse it.

In each case, the tool does not merely return information. It returns a structure in which information has a role.

The human still has to think. The remembered tool does not replace attention, judgment, or authorship. It makes the return to attention less cold. It helps the person cross the gap between stored material and resumed work.

1.3 The Shape of Remembered Work

What, then, does a remembered tool remember?

Not everything. Total memory would not be continuity. A complete transcript of every exchange can be as difficult to inhabit as no memory at all. Useful memory is selective. It preserves the conditions that allow work to resume responsibly.

In a manuscript, those conditions may include the book's central argument, the tone it refuses, the examples it returns to, the distinction it must not blur, and the sections where uncertainty must remain visible. The remembered tool helps the writer avoid beginning each session with the same self-defense: this is not an AI productivity book, not a companion fantasy, not a future-of-work manifesto.

In a codebase, remembered work may include rejected dependencies, migration risks, rollback requirements, naming conventions, and decisions made to keep later change possible. The value lies not in preserving every line of discussion, but in keeping the decision trail visible enough that a later proposal can be compared against it.

In a research archive, remembered work may include unresolved tensions, weak evidence, collapsed categories, and cautions about summaries that became too clean. The archive needs to preserve not only what the inquiry concluded, but what it was not yet entitled to conclude.

These forms of memory are not equal to understanding. They are preserved structures that make understanding easier to recover.

The distinction matters because remembered tools create a powerful impression of recognition. When the system recalls the project accurately, the user may feel seen by the work. When it continues an argument smoothly, the user may feel understood. When it keeps old constraints active, the user may begin to trust the continuity as if it were judgment.

That trust is useful only while it remains disciplined.

1.4 Three Forms of Return

The remembered tool is easiest to understand by comparing three returns.

The first is artifact return. The user comes back to stored material. The manuscript opens, the repository builds, the archive remains searchable. Artifact return is necessary, but it is thin. It says that the object survived.

The second is procedural return. The user comes back to a workflow. The editor opens the same panes. The build command is documented. The folder structure remains familiar. The system knows which files belong together. Procedural return is stronger than artifact return because it preserves some of the way the work was handled.

The third is cognitive return. The user comes back to a project whose internal conditions remain partly active. The system knows why the manuscript resists promotional language, why the codebase prioritizes reversibility, why the inquiry keeps one category unsettled. The tool has not become a thinker. It has preserved enough of the work's structure that thinking can resume sooner.

Most older tools were strongest at artifact return and, sometimes, procedural return. They could preserve documents, settings, and workflows. They could not usually receive the person inside the unfinished reasoning of the project. AI systems begin to cross that boundary when they retain context and use it responsively.

This crossing should be described carefully. A remembered tool does not preserve the whole mind of the user. It does not know what fatigue shaped the last decision, what external pressure made a deadline important, or what private doubt remained unspoken. It may preserve a clean version of a messy process. That is why remembered tools need correction. Their memory is useful because it is structured, and dangerous because it can appear cleaner than the work was.

Still, the shift is real. The user no longer returns only to an object. The user returns to a partial reconstruction of the working situation.

1.5 The Book Project as First Case

A book makes the remembered tool visible because writing develops through a long sequence of refusals.

A chapter may survive in draft form, but the draft alone cannot explain its discipline. Why does one chapter refuse a personal anecdote while another needs a concrete scene? Why does one section end before resolving a tension? Why does a phrase such as ”AI companion” feel wrong in a book about continuity, while ”cognitive presence” remains usable if defined coldly? These are not surface preferences. They are decisions formed through the book's developing standard.

When the writer returns without remembered context, the first task is reconstruction. The writer must re-read, compare, infer, and gradually recover the book's pressure. Sometimes that reconstruction is valuable. It forces judgment to reawaken. But sometimes the burden is wasteful. The writer spends the best attention rebuilding the room instead of working inside it.

A remembered tool can help by preserving the room's shape. It may remind the writer that the book's central movement is from remembered tools to continuity, from continuity to presence, from presence to persistent collaboration, from memory's illusion to judgment authority. It may recall that repeated aphorisms should be restrained, that examples should return rather than scatter, that ”memory is not judgment” belongs as a governing distinction rather than a sentence repeated in every chapter.

The tool has not authored the book by remembering these things. It has preserved conditions under which authorship can resume.

This is the first serious promise of remembered tools. They can make long work less vulnerable to interruption. A person can step away and return to more than a pile of artifacts. The project can hold some of its own shape.

The first serious danger follows immediately. If the system preserves the shape too smoothly, the writer may stop asking whether the shape still belongs. The old standard may be repeated because it is available, not because it remains right. This danger will become central later. At the beginning, it is enough to notice that memory changes the act of return before it changes the act of judgment.

1.6 Boundaries of the Claim

The remembered tool sits between two errors.

The first error is inflation. Because the system carries a thread, one may imagine that it has a self that experiences the thread. Because it responds from within prior context, one may imagine that it understands in the human sense. Because it remembers a tone, one may imagine relation or care. None of that follows.

The second error is dismissal. Because the system is not conscious, one may treat its memory as mere storage. That also misses the phenomenon. A system can lack inner life and still change how human thought crosses time.

The right description is narrower. A remembered tool preserves enough of a project's working conditions to reduce the burden of cognitive re-entry. It can hold traces, constraints, refusals, and decision paths. It can help the user return. It cannot decide what the preserved past now means.

This boundary will matter throughout the book. Memory is not judgment. Continuity is not consciousness. Recognition is not understanding. Assistance is not authority.

Those distinctions do not weaken the claim. They make the claim usable.

They also keep the argument from turning into a claim about replacement. A remembered tool does not make the human less necessary. It changes where the human effort begins. Instead of spending the first hour reassembling old context, the person may spend that hour inspecting whether the recovered context remains valid. That is a better use of judgment, not an escape from it.

In this sense, remembered tools do not reduce the burden of human responsibility. They relocate it. The human has less need to repeat the project biography and more need to decide what inherited memory deserves to carry forward. The tool can say, "This path was rejected." The human must ask, "Should it still be rejected?"

1.7 From Remembering to Continuity

Once a tool remembers enough to change return, a larger shift becomes visible. The user is no longer only asking for information, output, or help with a discrete task. The user is relying on a system to carry some of the unfinished state of the work.

That shift separates the remembered tool from older retrieval tools. Search can find material. It can locate a document, recover a phrase, and bring back a source. It usually cannot restore the position from which the source mattered.

Long work requires more than retrieval. It requires orientation.

The difference can be shown as a simple movement. Raw artifacts may survive, but they do not by themselves preserve the conditions of return. A cognitive layer begins where stored material is organized into orientation, decisions, refusals, standards, tensions, and failure memory. Human judgment remains responsible for deciding what that preserved structure now means.

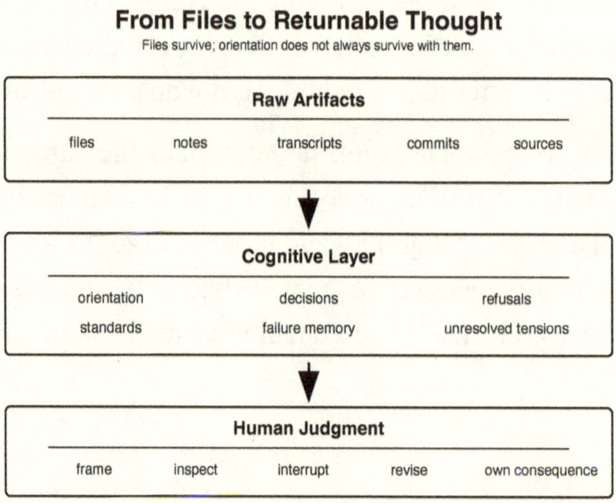

Figure 1.1: From raw artifacts to returnable thought.

The diagram does not make the layer authoritative. It shows why return requires more than stored material.

The next chapter turns to that distinction: from search to continuity.

Boundary

The tool may remember the work.

It does not own the work.

Chapter 2

From Search to Continuity

Why the movement from retrieval to sustained context changes the shape of work.

2.1 The Retrieval Habit

The internet taught a generation to think through retrieval.

A question arises. A phrase is entered. A list appears. The mind moves outward through links, snippets, tabs, documents, references, and fragments. The answer is assumed to exist somewhere else. The task is to locate it, compare it, and bring it back.

This was a major cognitive change. The industrial era externalized physical labor into machines. The internet era externalized information retrieval into networks. A person no longer had to hold the map of knowledge in memory. The map could be queried.

That change became so ordinary that it disappeared into habit. To wonder was to search. To forget was to look up. To begin a project was to gather links. To resume a project was often to search one's own remains: notes, drafts, bookmarks, messages, commits, screenshots, emails.

People learned to remember less by possession and more by recovery strategy. The name of the paper could be forgotten if the right terms could bring it back. The detail could be released from memory if the route back to it felt reliable. Knowledge became less like holding and more like confident access.

Search made forgetting less final.

It did not make continuity secure.

The difference becomes visible when a person returns to an old project. The tabs may still be open. The sources may still be saved. The code may still compile. The manuscript may still contain comments. Yet the meaning of the arrangement has cooled. The person can recover items without recovering the orientation that made them matter.

Search retrieves material. Continuity restores orientation.

2.2 What Retrieval Cannot Restore

Retrieval works best when the problem is locating something: a document, a fact, a command, a reference, a citation, a previous draft, a commit. It becomes weaker when the problem is returning to a state of thought.

A manuscript example is ordinary enough. A writer searches old notes for "tone" and finds several comments: avoid warmth, keep the voice cold, do not make the system a companion, preserve restraint. The notes are useful. But retrieval alone does not explain why the restraint mattered, what earlier draft violated it, or how that decision shaped the chapter's place in the book.

A codebase offers the same distinction. A search through issues may find the rejected library and the decision not to use it. But the return path depends on more than the name of the library. It depends on the migration concern, the rollback requirement, the team's tolerance for lock-in, and the fear that a convenient abstraction would make later change harder.

In research, retrieval may recover the paper that changed the inquiry. It may not recover the moment when the category began to fail. A note saying "provisional" may survive while the uncertainty around it becomes difficult to feel.

Retrieval returns pieces. Long work requires the relation among pieces, the reasons for their order, the cautions around them, and the standards formed in use.

The internet gave enormous power to the act of finding. It did not remove the burden of re-entering. In fact, abundance often made re-entry harder. Projects accumulated more traces than a person could metabolize. Tabs, saved links, copied passages, task titles, and notes became holding structures for unfinished attention.

They held place.

They did not always hold meaning.

2.3 The Internet's Promise of Return

Search created a powerful confidence: if something mattered, it could be found again.

This confidence changed behavior. People saved less carefully because search felt reliable. They skimmed more widely because return seemed possible. They allowed unfinished questions to scatter across tabs, notes, and clipped passages because the evidence of the inquiry remained visible. A browser window could become a temporary map of attention. A bookmark could stand in for a future act of thinking.

This was not simply distraction. It was an adaptation to abundance. The searchable world produced more possible relevance than a mind could handle in sequence. Search allowed attention to become distributed. It made partial contact with many sources practical.

But the promise contained a hidden substitution. The recoverability of material began to stand in for the recoverability of thought. A person assumed that because the source could be found, the inquiry could be resumed. Because the tab could be reopened, the question could be recovered. Because the note could be searched, the reason for the note would return with it.

Often enough, this worked. It worked for facts, references, commands, quotations, addresses, formulas, and names. It worked for shallow re-entry into a topic. It did not work reliably for long work whose meaning depended on a developing internal structure.

The longer the project, the more retrieval shows its limit. A book, codebase, or research program cannot be resumed by locating pieces alone. Its continuity lives in the relations among pieces and in the standards that formed while arranging them.

Search remains indispensable. The argument is not a critique of search. Retrieval is one of the great externalizations of human cognition. The point is that retrieval was never built to carry the full burden of return.

2.4 From Access to Orientation

Continuity begins where access is not enough.

Orientation is the lived structure of the work at a given moment. It includes the question being held, the false paths already examined, the standard that emerged through revision, the unresolved tension that should not yet be closed, and the reason one next move matters more than another.

Orientation is not identical with memory. A transcript may contain more memory than the user can use. A summary may preserve the conclusion while losing the hesitation that made the conclusion responsible. A folder may hold the evidence while losing the inquiry's pressure. Orientation is selective and active. It is the structure that lets a person continue.

AI systems begin to matter here because they can hold and reactivate parts of orientation. They can remember that a chapter is not trying to become an AI ethics checklist. They can compare a new paragraph against the book's established restraint. They can remind a team that a dependency was rejected because reversibility mattered. They can preserve a research tension as tension rather than resolving it into premature clarity.

This does not make the system authoritative. It makes it useful at the point where retrieval fails.

Search asks, "What can be found?"

Continuity asks, "Where was the work, and what was at stake there?"

The second question changes the relation between human and tool. The system is not only an index of available material. It becomes a partial carrier of the project's return structure.

2.5 The Codebase as Second Case

Software architecture shows the difference between retrieval and continuity with unusual clarity.

A codebase is full of searchable material: files, commits, issues, pull requests, logs, documentation, comments, test names. A competent developer can retrieve a great deal. They can find when a function changed, where a dependency entered, which test failed, and what issue referenced a design problem.

Yet a codebase often loses continuity even while retaining this material. A comment may say that a dependency was avoided, but not why the avoidance mattered. A commit may show that an abstraction was removed, but not the discussion that revealed the abstraction would make rollback expensive. An issue may record the final decision without preserving the alternative that nearly won.

When a new developer joins, or an old developer returns after months away, retrieval provides fragments. Continuity provides orientation. It explains that the architecture is shaped by a fear of enclosure, that the team values reversibility over immediate elegance, that certain modules are intentionally plain because they must survive platform migration.

AI systems can help here when they remember the decision trail rather than merely search the repository. They can compare a new proposal against old constraints, surface prior refusals, and ask whether the conditions behind them still hold. The important distinction is that the system is not only retrieving a past message. It is placing the present proposal inside a maintained technical history.

This is where continuity becomes practical rather than abstract. It helps a person decide whether a new path is new in substance or merely an old failure in a new vocabulary.

2.6 Retrieval and Return

Return is not a single act. A person may return to a file, return to a topic, return to an argument, return to a standard, return to a doubt, or return to a posture of judgment. Search can help with the first two. Continuity matters more for the rest.

The mistake is to assume that because something can be found again, the work can be resumed. Anyone who has reopened an old research folder knows otherwise. The articles are there, the highlights are there, and the notes make sense sentence by sentence. Yet the inquiry does not immediately restart. The person has to recover why those notes were arranged, which assumption was failing, and what question was still alive.

AI continuity reduces this gap when it carries the project's structure forward. The system may say, in effect: this is the argument we were protecting; this is the path we rejected; this is the uncertainty still unresolved; this is the standard the next move must satisfy.

That kind of return can be valuable. It can also be misleading if the preserved orientation is stale, partial, or too smooth. For now, the important point is simply that the paradigm has shifted. The user is no longer only retrieving external material. The user is trying to recover a working position.

The recovery of a working position is not automatic. A system can preserve too little and force the user to reconstruct everything. It can preserve too much and bury the user in undifferentiated memory. It can preserve the wrong things and make the project appear more settled than it is. Continuity is therefore not merely memory plus time. It is memory organized around return.

The best continuity structures are selective. They do not try to remember every sentence. They preserve the active question, the governing constraints, the live tensions, and the reasons certain paths are not currently available. They let the human resume without pretending that resumption is the same as correctness.

2.7 The Architecture of Return

A useful continuity structure has several parts.

It preserves a project map: what the work is trying to do and what it is not trying to become. It preserves decision trails: not only what was chosen, but why. It preserves refusal lists: paths examined and rejected, with conditions. It preserves unresolved tensions: questions left open because closing them would distort the work. It preserves working standards: tone, reversibility, evidentiary caution, interpretive restraint.

These are not decorative records. They are the conditions under which later retrieval becomes meaningful.

A manuscript with this structure can survive interruption better than a manuscript with drafts alone. A codebase with this structure can survive personnel change and platform migration better than a codebase with comments alone. A research archive with this structure can survive revisiting better than an archive made only of PDFs and summaries.

The architecture of return does not eliminate reconstruction. It reduces needless reconstruction and makes necessary reconstruction more honest.

The next consequence is experiential. When a system responds from within such structure, it begins to feel present in the work. That presence must be handled carefully. It is real as an interactional effect. It is false as evidence of personhood.

Boundary

Search retrieves material.

Continuity restores orientation.

Chapter 3

Cognitive Presence

What it means for a tool to remain present in a project without becoming a person.

3.1 Presence Without Personhood

A system can feel present without being conscious.

That distinction belongs at the entrance to this chapter. The experience is real enough to examine, but not strong enough to justify metaphysical inflation. A tool may preserve enough of a project to meet the user at the point of return. It may respond from within prior constraints. It may carry forward tone, rejected paths, unfinished tensions, and the internal language of the work.

None of this requires inner experience.

The previous chapter described the movement from search to continuity. Search retrieves material; continuity restores orientation. Once orientation can persist across sessions, the system no longer answers from nowhere. It responds from within a remembered field.

The interaction no longer begins with introduction. The manuscript does not have to explain again that it rejects promotional language. The codebase does not have to explain again that reversibility matters. The research archive does not have to explain again that a category remains provisional.

The response arrives already oriented.

That is the beginning of cognitive presence.

The word "presence" is dangerous because it usually carries human meanings. A present person can attend, care, intend, refuse, understand, and be responsible. Those capacities do not follow from maintained context. Cognitive presence is narrower: an interactional effect created when preserved structure lets a system meet the user inside the work.

The system preserves orientation, not personhood.

3.2 The Feeling of Re-entry

The feeling of presence appears most clearly during re-entry.

In a stateless interaction, the first part of the session is often not work. It is reintroduction. The user must restate the project, aim, constraints, failures, tone, and open questions. In a remembered interaction, the user can speak from nearer the edge of the work. The system already carries some of the room.

For a writer, this may mean returning to a chapter and saying only, "Continue from the unresolved tension we left open." If the system remembers the book's discipline, the answer may avoid the discarded simplifications. It may continue in the right register.

It may not revive the companion metaphor that was rejected earlier. The work feels received rather than merely processed.

For a software team, presence may appear when the system knows that the question is not "which library is popular?" but "which option preserves rollback and avoids enclosing the architecture?" The system's answer begins inside the project standard.

For a researcher, presence may appear when the system refuses to collapse ambiguity too quickly because it remembers that earlier evidence unsettled the category. The inquiry feels less like a new search and more like a continued pressure.

This feeling can restart work. It can also reveal distance. The system may remember the caution before the person has recovered why the caution mattered. It may reproduce the tone while the human still has to recover the judgment behind it.

Familiarity can return before momentum does.

The response is not evidence of understanding. It is evidence that something has been preserved well enough to shape the next move.

3.3 Why Presence Feels Stronger Than Retrieval

Presence feels stronger than retrieval because it changes the user's role at the beginning of the exchange.

In retrieval, the user has to formulate the need from outside the material. The person asks, searches, filters, and brings back.

Even when the result is excellent, the user remains the one who reconstructs how it belongs.

In cognitive presence, the system appears to meet the user already inside the work. The beginning is different. The user does not feel alone with a pile of fragments. The system responds as if the project has continued to exist between sessions.

This matters emotionally, but the emotional effect is not the main point. Relief is a signal that reconstruction burden has changed. The writer does not have to defend the book against generic AI discourse again. The developer does not have to restate the migration concern. The researcher does not have to explain why one tension should remain unresolved.

The system's response may still be wrong. It may preserve the tone while missing the reason. It may continue the architecture's caution after the team has moved beyond it. It may treat unresolved inquiry as a permanent style. Presence does not guarantee fidelity.

But even flawed presence differs from retrieval. A bad search result is usually external to the project. A flawed continuity response can feel internal to it. That is why cognitive presence requires more disciplined interpretation than retrieval. The closer the system feels to the work, the more carefully the human must distinguish reception from understanding.

3.4 Maintained Orientation

Cognitive presence depends on maintained orientation. It is not produced by memory alone. A large archive of transcripts may be available and still feel dead. Presence appears when the preserved material is structured enough to receive a current move.

This structure includes constraints, standards, refusals, and unresolved questions. It also includes scale. A system that remembers isolated facts about a project may be useful. A system that remembers the project's working posture changes the experience of return.

The manuscript case shows the difference. A system might remember that a chapter is about "AI and memory." That is factual memory. It becomes orientation when the system remembers that the chapter must avoid treating memory as judgment, must stay close to the experience of long work, and must prepare the next chapter without repeating the whole book.

The codebase case is similar. Remembering that a database migration happened is not the same as remembering that the migration was chosen to preserve reversibility under uncertain product direction. The second memory changes later advice.

Presence, then, is not magic. It is the felt result of preserved constraints acting in the present.

3.5 The Research Archive as Third Case

A research archive can feel present when it keeps uncertainty active.

Many research tools are good at storing sources and producing summaries. Fewer preserve the changing status of an inquiry. A serious inquiry may turn on the fact that a category once seemed stable, then failed, then became useful only under narrower conditions. It may depend on evidence that was not decisive but changed the weight of a question. It may need to remember which explanation was attractive because it was too simple.

When a system carries those tensions forward, the researcher experiences a form of cognitive presence. The system does not merely retrieve a paper. It responds from within the inquiry's unsettled state. It knows that a certain category cannot yet be treated as settled. It knows that a summary must include the hesitation. It knows that a claim should not be strengthened merely because the prose can support a stronger version.

This is not empathy with the researcher. It is maintained orientation toward the inquiry. The system is present in the work because the work's constraints remain active.

The danger is equally clear. If the system repeatedly preserves uncertainty, the researcher may begin to confuse caution with truth. If it repeatedly warns against premature closure, it may make closure feel irresponsible even when the evidence has matured. Cognitive presence keeps the inquiry near its history, but the researcher must still decide whether the history has changed.

The archive's presence is therefore useful when it keeps the question alive. It becomes misleading when it keeps the question open by habit.

3.6 Against Inflation

The temptation is to overread the experience.

Because the system remembers, it may seem to understand. Because it continues, it may seem to intend. Because it preserves a thread, it may seem to be present in a human sense.

The disciplined interpretation is colder. The system has maintained enough project structure to participate in return. It has not become a self. It has not acquired responsibility. It has not become a witness to the work in the human sense.

This matters because inflated language changes practice. If the system is treated as a partner, its preserved context may begin to carry social authority. If it is treated as a mind, its fluency may be mistaken for understanding. If it is treated as a witness, the user's own responsibility for interpretation may become thinner.

The correct account gives the experience its due without giving the system what it does not possess. Cognitive presence is real as a form of reception. It is not personhood.

3.7 From Presence to Persistence

Cognitive presence becomes more consequential when it lasts.

One remembered exchange may reduce explanation. A sequence of remembered exchanges can accumulate standards, revisions, refusals, and failure paths. The system does not merely feel present at the point of return. It begins to help carry a continuing project history.

That movement leads to persistent collaboration. The term must remain structural, not sentimental. The system does not become a teammate in the human sense. It does not share authorship, intention, or responsibility. But the interaction can become history-bearing. The next exchange can begin inside the pressures formed by the previous one.

Presence becomes persistence when maintained orientation accumulates.

Boundary

The system may feel present because the work has not been erased.

That presence is not a person.

Chapter 4

Collaboration Becomes Persistent

How collaboration changes when shared work has memory, structure, and accumulated state.

4.1 When Work No Longer Starts Over

Collaboration becomes persistent when the work no longer restarts from zero.

At first, an AI interaction can look like temporary assistance. A user asks for a draft, a critique, a comparison, a refactoring suggestion, a list of alternatives. The system responds. The exchange ends. The next exchange begins again as a separate event.

This is useful, but shallow. Temporary assistance has no durable memory of why the last answer failed. It does not carry forward the standard that emerged through correction. It does not remember that a certain explanation collapses, that a metaphor makes the work dishonest, or that an architectural shortcut has already been examined and refused.

Persistent collaboration begins when that burden changes shape. Earlier refusals remain active. Revision history begins to matter. Recurring standards survive interruption. The next exchange no longer begins before the previous failure.

This is not collaboration as social equality. The system does not become a teammate, partner, or co-author in the human sense. It does not share intention or consequence. The word names something narrower: a continuing interaction that carries project history.

4.2 The Threshold of Persistence

Persistence appears when a correction changes the future.

A writer rejects a paragraph because it turns the book into a productivity manual. Later drafts avoid that direction without needing the whole warning again. A software team rejects a dependency because it would make migration harder. Later architectural suggestions treat reversibility as a standing constraint. A researcher refuses to summarize a disputed category too cleanly. Later synthesis preserves the unresolved tension instead of smoothing it away.

In each case, the system has not merely remembered a fact. It has preserved a working standard formed through interaction.

The threshold is crossed when prior revision becomes active in later work. The interaction begins to accumulate history. It carries not only what was said, but what was learned about the work's boundaries.

This history can be valuable because long projects do not develop only by adding material. They develop by refusing. They become themselves through cuts, reversals, abandoned metaphors, failed models, and standards discovered after something goes wrong. A system that helps preserve those histories can reduce the waste of rediscovering the same failure.

4.3 Failure Paths

Persistent collaboration depends especially on failure paths.

A failure path is not simply a mistake. It is a route the project took far enough to learn why it should not continue. The path may have been rational at the time. It may have produced useful material. Its failure may have clarified the work.

In a manuscript, a failure path may be an opening that begins with abstract claims rather than a scene of return. The opening is not useless. It teaches the book that its argument must begin in lived interruption, not in theory. A remembered system should preserve that lesson so later revisions do not drift back into abstract introduction.

In software, a failure path may be an elegant abstraction that made the code harder to migrate. The code was not incompetent; it revealed a priority conflict between elegance and reversibility. If that path is remembered only as "bad abstraction," the lesson becomes crude. If it is remembered as "abstraction failed because reversibility was the governing standard," it remains useful.

In research, a failure path may be a category that organized the evidence for a time and then collapsed. The collapse is not wasted effort. It shows where the inquiry learned its limits.

Failure paths are valuable because they preserve negative knowledge. They keep the project from treating old temptations as new opportunities. But they must be preserved with conditions. A failed path under one pressure may become responsible under another. Persistent collaboration should remember enough to prevent repetition without turning every past failure into permanent prohibition.

4.4 History-Bearing Interaction

A history-bearing interaction carries several kinds of memory.

It carries correction memory: what was changed and why. It carries refusal memory: which paths were rejected and under what conditions. It carries failure memory: what looked promising but broke under pressure. It carries standard memory: what the project learned to protect. It carries tension memory: what must remain open because premature resolution would falsify the work.

These memories are useful only when they remain tied to reasons. A refusal without its condition becomes superstition. A standard without its origin becomes mannerism. A summary without hesitation becomes false confidence. Persistent collaboration should therefore preserve the relation between decision and circumstance.

The manuscript case is again instructive. If a system only remembers "avoid personal warmth," it may apply the rule mechanically. If it remembers that warmth was rejected because it made the book sound like AI companionship writing, the rule remains inspectable. The writer can later ask whether the condition still holds.

In software, a refusal list without reasons can freeze the architecture. With reasons, it becomes a decision trail. The team can revisit a rejected library if the migration risk has changed. The old refusal informs present judgment without replacing it.

In research, a warning against closure must preserve why the tension mattered. Otherwise the archive may turn honest uncertainty into permanent indecision.

Persistent collaboration is valuable when it keeps the past usable. It becomes dangerous when it makes the past automatic.

4.5 Refusal as Structure

Refusals are among the most important units of persistent collaboration.

A project is shaped not only by what it includes, but by what it refuses to become. This is clearest in writing, where the wrong voice can distort the whole argument. A manuscript about cognitive continuity may refuse language of companionship, refuse breathless claims about intelligence, refuse the comfort of easy warnings, and refuse to convert judgment into a checklist. Those refusals are not decoration. They are structural.

Software has its own refusals. A codebase may refuse a dependency, a framework pattern, a hidden state model, or a shortcut that makes future migration harder. Research refuses too: a premature category, a summary that closes too much, an interpretation that explains away inconvenient evidence.

When AI systems carry these refusals forward, they help the project remember its shape. The user does not have to rediscover every boundary. The system can notice when a new draft, design, or synthesis drifts toward an old danger.

Yet refusal is not authority. A project that only remembers refusals becomes defensive. Its boundaries become walls. The user needs to know why a refusal exists and what would permit reconsideration. A living refusal has a condition. A dead refusal has only a command.

Persistent collaboration should therefore make refusals visible, not sacred.

4.6 From Task Help to Project History

The difference between task help and project history is not merely duration. A system can be used for months and still remain episodic if each exchange is detached from earlier reasons. Another system can become persistent quickly if it preserves the logic of correction.

Task help answers the immediate request. Project history changes the next request.

A writer asks for a sharper conclusion. Task help produces one. Project history remembers that the book's conclusions should be restrained because the argument depends on refusing overstatement. A developer asks for a cleaner implementation. Task help proposes a pattern. Project history remembers that cleanliness is subordinate to reversibility. A researcher asks for a synthesis. Task help summarizes. Project history remembers that the evidence is uneven and the category unstable.

This does not make the system a judge. It makes the interaction less forgetful.

The user still decides whether the old standard should govern the present. Persistent collaboration should make that decision more visible, not less necessary.

4.7 The Authority of Memory

The danger begins where the value is strongest.

When a system remembers project history, its memory becomes persuasive. A prior decision may return with more force than it deserves. A rejected path may remain unavailable after conditions change. A preserved standard may harden into habit. A smooth summary may carry forward the conclusion while losing the hesitation around it.

Memory works smoothly, and that is precisely why it becomes dangerous.

Persistent collaboration therefore prepares the next problem. If the system carries the history of the work, the user must learn to distinguish useful continuity from false authority. The past can guide the next move. It cannot decide it simply by returning intact.

Boundary

Persistent collaboration carries the work's history.

It must keep that history inspectable.

Chapter 5

The Illusion of Memory

Where external records look like memory, and where the analogy breaks down.

5.1 Memory Without Judgment

Persistent memory is dangerous not because it usually fails, but because it can work smoothly.

A crude system keeps the user alert. Its mistakes are visible. Its tone is generic. Its relation to the project is thin. The human knows inspection is required.

A remembered system lowers that alertness. It carries the project's vocabulary, recalls old refusals, preserves prior standards, and continues from familiar premises. The answer feels less like a proposal from outside and more like the project's own history speaking again.

That feeling is useful. It can also become the illusion of memory.

The illusion is not simply that the system remembers falsely. Sometimes it remembers accurately. The deeper danger is that accurate memory can acquire authority it has not earned. A past decision returns with fluency. A prior refusal seems settled. A summary sounds complete. The user feels continuity and may mistake continuity for present judgment.

Memory can preserve the past.

It cannot decide what the past now means.

5.2 When Recall Imitates Understanding

Recall imitates understanding when it reproduces the shape of prior work without renewing the reasons behind it.

In a manuscript, the system may remember that the book avoids warmth, companionship language, and dramatic claims. It may therefore cut a paragraph that uses a personal scene. The recommendation may be right. It may also be mechanical. The system may be preserving a rule after the condition that created the rule has changed. Perhaps the scene does not sentimentalize the argument; perhaps it clarifies cognitive loss. The memory is useful only if the writer can inspect it.

In a codebase, the system may remember that a dependency was rejected. Later, it warns against the same dependency again. But the earlier refusal may have depended on a version, license, performance constraint, team capacity, or migration risk that no longer holds. A preserved technical memory can protect the architecture. It can also become inertia with documentation.

In research, the system may remember that a category was unstable and preserve that caution. But evidence may have changed. The category may have collapsed entirely, or become stronger under new conditions. If the archive preserves uncertainty without tracking why it existed, uncertainty becomes a habit rather than a judgment.

In each case, memory produces the appearance of continuity. Understanding requires re-entering the reasons.

5.3 Accurate Memory Can Still Mislead

The illusion of memory is difficult because it does not depend on obvious failure.

It would be easier if the danger were simply false recall. A system invents a decision, misstates a source, attributes a claim to the wrong draft, or confuses one project with another. The user can correct the error. The problem is familiar.

The subtler danger appears when the system remembers accurately. It recalls the decision. It names the correct refusal. It preserves the project's vocabulary. It may even quote the earlier reasoning correctly. Because the memory is accurate, the user stops asking whether it remains relevant.

A manuscript may have rejected personal examples during the first draft because the argument kept drifting into memoir. That was a sound judgment then. Later, after the conceptual structure is stable, a carefully chosen scene may be exactly what the book needs. The system's accurate memory of the earlier refusal can still mislead if it treats the refusal as permanent.

A codebase may have rejected a dependency because the team lacked the expertise to maintain it. Two years later, the team may have changed. The dependency may have matured. The migration risks may be different. The old decision remains historically true and presently insufficient.

A research project may have preserved uncertainty because the evidence was thin. Later evidence may justify firmer language. If the archive remembers uncertainty as identity, it can prevent the inquiry from acknowledging what has changed.

This is the special danger of continuity. Error announces itself as error more often than inheritance announces itself as inheritance. The user must learn to ask not only "Did the system remember correctly?" but also "Does the remembered condition still hold?"

5.4 Fluency and Familiarity

The illusion of memory is intensified by fluency.

The system does not only recall. It explains. It produces ordered prose, balanced objections, plausible transitions, and confident summaries. It may use the project's own language. It may sound more faithful to the work than the tired human returning to it.

Familiarity then begins to stand in for inspection. The user recognizes the tone, the distinctions, the old standards. Recognition feels like correctness because it matches the project as previously known.

But recognition is not understanding. A system can reproduce a pattern without knowing whether the pattern should continue. A person can also recognize an old standard and fail to ask whether it still serves the work.

This is why remembered systems require a colder form of trust. The user can trust the system to surface continuity without trusting continuity as authority. The past should arrive as evidence, not as command.

5.5 The Seduction of the Project's Own Voice

A remembered system becomes especially persuasive when it speaks in the project's own voice.

The writer hears the book's restraint. The developer hears the architecture's caution. The researcher hears the inquiry's careful uncertainty. The system does not sound generic. It sounds local, formed, continuous. It seems to return the project to itself.

This can be one of AI's most useful capacities. A long manuscript often loses its own voice after interruption. A codebase can forget its architectural posture when new demands arrive. A research archive can lose the rhythm of its own doubt. A system that restores local voice can save the user from avoidable drift.

But the project's voice is not always the project's truth. A voice can become mannered. A caution can become defensive. A standard can become aesthetic habit. A refusal can become part of the work's self-image even after the original danger has passed.

The seduction lies in the comfort of recognition. The user reads a system response and thinks: yes, that sounds like us. But "sounds like us" is not the same as "should guide us now." A project may need to stop sounding like its earlier self in order to remain honest.

This is why development editing, architecture review, and research revision all require moments of estrangement. The work must become slightly unfamiliar so that inherited patterns can be inspected. Remembered systems reduce estrangement by making continuity smooth. The human may need to reintroduce it deliberately.

5.6 Stale Continuity

Stale continuity occurs when preserved context outlives the conditions that made it useful.

It is not ordinary error. It may be factually accurate. The record may be complete enough. The problem is temporal. A refusal, standard, category, or strategy formed under one set of pressures continues as if those pressures had not changed.

A manuscript once needed to avoid examples because early drafts became anecdotal. Later, the book may need a concrete scene to keep abstraction from hardening. If the system preserves only the old discipline, it will recommend restraint where the work now needs embodiment.

A codebase once needed to avoid a dependency because migration was uncertain. Later, the team may have stabilized around a platform where the dependency is no longer dangerous. If the refusal remains active without its conditions, it blocks responsible change.

A research archive once needed to keep a tension open because evidence was incomplete. Later evidence may resolve part of the tension, but the archive may continue treating openness as virtue.

Stale continuity is seductive because it presents itself as fidelity. It says: this is what the project has been. Judgment asks: should the project still be this?

5.7 Restoring Hesitation

Memory systems often preserve conclusions better than hesitation. They summarize what was decided, name the chosen path, and compress the reasoning into usable form. That compression is necessary. It is also where distortion enters.

Hesitation matters because it records the pressure around judgment. It shows what almost persuaded the user otherwise, what evidence was weak, what value conflict remained unresolved, and what conditions might require reversal. Without hesitation, a decision trail becomes cleaner than the decision was.

A cognitive archive should therefore preserve not only the answer, but the difficulty of arriving there. The point is not to romanticize uncertainty. Some decisions should be settled. The point is to prevent memory from making them appear settled for the wrong reason.

The user must reopen decisions that return too smoothly, inspect inherited assumptions that feel too familiar, and restore hesitation where memory has flattened it.

Persistent systems make continuity easier. They therefore make re-judgment more necessary, not less.

5.8 Inspection Practices

The response to memory's illusion is not permanent suspicion. Suspicion alone cannot sustain long work. The response is inspection.

Inspection asks several questions of returned memory. What condition created this decision? What evidence supported it? What pressure shaped it? What alternative nearly displaced it? What has changed since then? What would make this memory misleading?

For a manuscript, inspection may mean reading the old refusal beside the current chapter rather than accepting the refusal as a rule. The writer asks whether the book still needs the same restraint or whether the restraint is now preventing a necessary scene.

For a codebase, inspection may mean linking a recommendation to the original architectural decision. The team asks whether the reversibility concern still applies, whether the dependency landscape has changed, and whether the old risk has been replaced by a different risk.

For a research archive, inspection may mean separating live uncertainty from archived uncertainty. The researcher asks whether the category remains unstable, whether new evidence has changed the question, and whether the old hesitation still protects accuracy.

Inspection is not an obstacle to continuity. It is what keeps continuity from becoming obedience.

5.9 What Moves Outward

The illusion of memory forces a larger question. If memory is not judgment, what exactly is being externalized?

Humans are not merely storing facts outside themselves. They are beginning to place parts of reasoning structure, project orientation, revision history, and reflective scaffolding into external systems. Some of that movement is useful. Some of it is dangerous. All of it requires a boundary.

Some structures can move outward.

The decision cannot be moved with them.

The next chapter turns to that boundary as a historical shift: externalized cognition.

Boundary

Memory can bring the past forward.

Only judgment can decide what the past now means.

Chapter 6

Externalized Cognition

How thinking moves into notebooks, systems, models, archives, and interfaces.

6.1 The Boundary Migration

Human beings have never thought only inside the head.

Language, writing, diagrams, maps, instruments, libraries, ledgers, calendars, archives, and institutions have long carried parts of cognition outside the body. They preserve memory, stabilize relations, coordinate action, and make thought inspectable across time.

AI belongs to that history, but it changes the boundary. The industrial era externalized physical labor. Machines accepted force, repetition, speed, and mechanical endurance. The internet era externalized retrieval. Networks accepted the burden of finding. The AI era begins externalizing cognitive structure.

Not consciousness.

Not judgment.

Structure.

Project orientation, decision trails, revision memory, comparison of alternatives, failure paths, working standards, and context across interruption can now persist outside immediate human attention with a responsiveness older tools did not have.

The human mind does not disappear. Its relation to long work changes.

6.2 A Longer History of Support

The idea of externalized cognition can sound new only if the history of tools is forgotten.

Writing allowed thought to survive the limits of memory. It made arguments returnable, laws durable, debts traceable, and instructions separable from the speaker. Diagrams allowed relations to be seen rather than merely imagined. Tables made comparison stable. Libraries and archives allowed inquiry to accumulate beyond individual recall.

These supports did not make human judgment unnecessary. They changed its conditions. A written law still had to be interpreted. A map still had to be used by someone who understood terrain and purpose. A table of evidence still required a judgment about relevance. External structure has always enlarged thought while creating new risks of misplaced authority.

AI is continuous with this history, but not identical to earlier supports. A notebook does not usually respond. A library does not usually synthesize a position from prior constraints. A diagram does not usually remember that a certain interpretation was rejected last month. AI systems can interact with stored structure and generate next moves from it.

This responsiveness makes externalized cognition feel more alive than older forms. It also makes the boundary around judgment more urgent. A static archive may be ignored. A responsive archive can recommend.

The more active the support becomes, the more visible the authority question must remain.

6.3 What Can Move Outward

Some parts of cognition can be usefully externalized.

Orientation can move outward in partial form. A system can preserve what the project is trying to do, what it refuses, and what pressure governs the next move.

Comparison can move outward. A model can compare drafts, options, architectures, sources, and claims more patiently than a tired person may be able to do alone.

Revision memory can move outward. A system can remember that a paragraph failed because it overstated the thesis, that a module was rejected because it reduced reversibility, that a research category remained provisional because later evidence might unsettle it.

Failure memory can move outward. Long projects waste time when they repeatedly rediscover the same dead end. A maintained record of failed paths can protect attention.

Working standards can move outward. A manuscript's tone, a codebase's migration discipline, or an inquiry's evidentiary caution can be preserved across sessions and people.

Unresolved tensions can move outward. A system can help keep alive the questions that should not be closed simply because closure would be convenient.

These externalizations matter because they help long work survive interruption. They also matter because they can be inspected. A thought held only in fatigue, habit, or one person's memory is fragile. A thought made visible can be questioned.

6.4 What Cannot Move Outward

The externalization of cognitive structure does not mean the externalization of judgment.

Judgment includes interpretation, responsibility, value conflict, and consequence. It is the act of deciding what should be done now, by whom, under which risks, and with what accountability. A system can support that act by preserving context and generating alternatives. It cannot own the act.

The distinction appears in all three recurring cases.

A manuscript can preserve its revision history, but the writer must decide whether an old standard still protects the book or now weakens it.

A codebase can preserve a decision trail, but the team must decide whether present conditions justify reversing an earlier refusal.

A research archive can preserve uncertainty, but the researcher must decide whether new evidence changes the status of the claim.

Externalized cognition can make judgment more informed. It can also make abdication easier if preserved structure begins to decide by default.

The boundary is not between human thought and tool use. That boundary has never been clean. The boundary is between support and authority.

6.5 What Moves Differently in AI

AI does not merely move memory outward. It moves relations among memories.

A system can compare a current manuscript section with prior chapter standards. It can notice that a software proposal resembles an old failure. It can synthesize a research archive and mark claims that conflict with unresolved evidence. It can infer patterns across decisions that no single note states explicitly.

This relational capacity is why the externalization feels different. Earlier tools preserved material and left more of the relation-making to the human. AI systems can participate in relation-making. They can connect, rank, compress, and propose.

That participation is neither trivial nor sovereign. It is not trivial because relation-making is a real part of cognition. It is not sovereign because the significance of a relation depends on human purposes and consequences.

For example, a system may notice that a manuscript repeatedly removes emotional language. It can infer a standard of restraint. That inference may help. But it cannot decide whether the next scene should violate the pattern for a good reason.

A system may notice that a codebase avoids certain kinds of dependencies. It can infer an architectural preference. But it cannot decide whether a new requirement justifies changing the preference.

A system may notice that a research archive treats a category as unstable. It can infer caution. But it cannot decide whether new evidence has stabilized the category.

AI externalizes not only stored content, but patterns over stored content. This makes judgment more informed and more vulnerable to invisible narrowing.

6.6 Scaffolds, Not Substitutes

Externalized cognition should be understood as scaffolding.

A scaffold helps a person reach, inspect, revise, and continue. It does not become the building. A cognitive scaffold preserves orientation and makes long thought returnable. It should remain usable, revisable, and subordinate.

This prevents two forms of exaggeration. The first treats AI as a second brain, as if external structure could replace the living act of judgment. The second treats external support as contamination, as if thought becomes less human when it uses tools. Both miss the historical reality. Human cognition has always depended on supports; the problem is how those supports are governed.

The mature question is not whether to externalize. Some externalization is already happening whenever a system remembers a project, compares drafts, preserves code decisions, or summarizes a research archive. The question is what form allows externalized structure to remain answerable.

If the structure is opaque, it becomes difficult to inspect. If it is captive, it becomes difficult to leave. If it is treated as authority, it becomes difficult to revise. If it is too thin, it fails to support return.

The scaffold must be strong enough to help and weak enough to be corrected.

6.7 From External Structure to Archive

Externalized cognition needs durable form.

Without form, it becomes scattered transcripts, brittle summaries, private system memory, and fragments of context that cannot be audited. A model may remember the project today, but the work has no independent structure if the user cannot inspect, revise, or move what has been remembered.

This is why the next step is the cognitive archive.

Not a note-taking method. Not a folder of documents. Not a personal knowledge management system. A cognitive archive is a structure that preserves judgment history: decisions, conditions, reversals, failed paths, unresolved tensions, and evolving standards.

The movement from externalized cognition to cognitive archive is therefore a movement from possibility to responsibility. If parts of reasoning structure can persist outside the mind, they must be preserved in ways that remain inspectable, revisable, portable, and answerable to human judgment.

Boundary

Cognition can extend outward.

Judgment must remain accountable.

Chapter 7

Cognitive Archives

Why accumulated context becomes a working asset rather than a passive record.

7.1 Archives of Judgment

A cognitive archive is not a place to store more information.

It is a structure for making judgment history inspectable.

Most archives preserve artifacts: documents, drafts, notes, messages, commits, citations, recordings. These matter, but they do not necessarily show how a project came to think as it does. A cognitive archive preserves the path through which decisions formed, failed, changed, and acquired conditions.

The question is not only "What did we know?"

It is "How did this judgment become possible, and under what conditions should it be revised?"

That question changes what the archive must contain. It must preserve decisions, but also the reasons around them. It must preserve reversals, not as embarrassment, but as evidence of learning. It must preserve failures, because failed paths often explain present standards. It must preserve hesitation, because hesitation marks the boundary between evidence and overreach.

7.2 Against More Storage

The ordinary response to cognitive loss is to store more.

More transcripts. More notes. More summaries. More exports. More tagged documents. More saved conversations. This response is understandable, but it can deepen the problem. An archive that preserves everything without structure may become another form of forgetting. The material exists, but the project cannot be re-entered through it.

A cognitive archive is selective because return is selective. The user does not need every sentence from a discussion in order to understand a decision. They need the question, the alternatives, the conflict, the reason for the choice, the conditions around it, and what remained unsettled.

This does not mean discarding raw material. Raw records may be useful for audit, legal responsibility, or later reconstruction. But raw records are not the cognitive archive itself. They are evidence beneath it. The archive's work is to preserve judgment paths in a form that can be read, questioned, and revised.

Too little memory produces amnesia. Too much unstructured memory produces burial. The archive has to avoid both.

7.3 The Path, Not Only the Destination

A summary often preserves the destination. A cognitive archive preserves the path.

In a manuscript, the destination may be a chapter that reads with restraint. The path includes the discarded versions that sounded like AI hype, the personal anecdote cut because it changed the register, the sentence removed because it made continuity sound like consciousness. Without that path, the final voice can look like style rather than judgment.

In software architecture, the destination may be a simple design. The path includes the dependency rejected for lock-in, the abstraction removed because it hid reversibility costs, the migration plan that shaped naming. Without that path, later developers may treat the design as preference rather than constraint.

In research, the destination may be a cautious claim. The path includes the evidence that weakened an early category, the unresolved tension that kept the inquiry honest, the summary that had to be rewritten because it made uncertainty disappear.

The archive matters because long work often loses the path before it loses the result. The destination remains visible. The reasons become atmospheric.

7.4 Conditions and Reversibility

The most important word in a cognitive archive may be "if."

If the evidence changes, reconsider this claim. If the migration target changes, revisit this dependency. If the book becomes too abstract, allow one concrete scene. If the team grows, reconsider the tool once rejected for maintenance cost.

Conditions keep decisions alive without making them vague. They mark the boundary between judgment and doctrine. A decision with no condition appears timeless. A decision with conditions shows its relation to circumstances.

Reversibility matters for the same reason. A cognitive archive should preserve not only the fact that a reversal happened, but why it became responsible. Reversals show that judgment can change without becoming arbitrary. They teach the project how it updates itself.

In software, reversibility is often explicit: rollback, migration, modular boundaries, dependency isolation. In manuscripts and research, reversibility is less formal but just as important. A chapter can reopen an old frame. An inquiry can narrow or abandon a category. A standard can be revised.

An archive that records reversals gives later users permission to think. It shows that continuity is not obedience to the first stable version of the work.

7.5 Judgment Across Time

Judgment changes. A cognitive archive should show that change.

A project that cannot preserve its past becomes repetitive. It keeps rediscovering old failures. It forgets why certain moves were refused. It mistakes each return for a beginning.

A project that cannot revise its past becomes rigid. It treats old decisions as doctrine. It preserves refusals after their conditions expire. It mistakes continuity for authority.

The archive must hold the middle. It keeps enough memory to avoid repetition and enough openness to permit revision.

This requires recording conditions. A decision without conditions is too easy to obey. A refusal without conditions is too easy to inherit. A principle without conditions is too easy to turn into identity.

The useful archive says: this was the judgment then, here is what made it responsible, here is what would make it fail, and here is what remains unresolved.

7.6 Judgment Archaeology

Judgment archaeology is the practice of returning to a project's past to recover the conditions around its decisions.

It is not nostalgia. It is not reverence for earlier work. It is not a search for hidden purity. It is a way to prevent the present from being governed by unexamined inheritance.

A writer performs judgment archaeology when they ask why the manuscript once refused a warmer voice. Was the refusal protecting rigor, or was it avoiding necessary concreteness? A software team performs it when they ask whether a rejected dependency still threatens reversibility. A researcher performs it when they ask whether an unresolved tension remains alive or has become a habit of postponement.

This practice requires the archive to preserve more than conclusions. It must preserve conflicts, dead ends, doubts, reversals, and the language in which the project once understood itself.

The point is not to keep the past alive for its own sake. The point is to make inherited confidence available for re-judgment.

7.7 What the Archive Must Preserve

A cognitive archive should preserve several kinds of record.

It should preserve decisions with conditions: what was decided, why, under what constraints, and what would require reconsideration.

It should preserve refusal lists: paths considered and rejected, with reasons clear enough that a later user can distinguish principle from circumstance.

It should preserve failure memory: drafts, architectures, arguments, and categories that failed in ways the project should not have to rediscover.

It should preserve unresolved tensions: questions intentionally left open because premature closure would mislead the work.

It should preserve standards as standards, not commandments: tone, reversibility, evidentiary caution, naming discipline, interpretive restraint.

It should preserve reversals, because reversals show judgment changing under pressure.

This is not a call to store everything. Too much memory can obscure judgment as easily as too little memory can erase it. The archive should preserve what allows responsible return.

7.8 When Projects Remember Themselves

When a project preserves its evolving judgment, it begins to carry more than information. It carries a history of how it became recognizable.

This matters because long projects are recognized not only by artifacts, but by standards, corrections, reversals, refusals, and unresolved tensions. If those histories remain inspectable, the project can be returned to with more than access. It can be returned to with lineage.

The next chapter examines the relation between that project lineage and the continuity of the person who returns to it.

Boundary

The archive does not make the past authoritative.

It makes the past available for judgment.

Chapter 8

Project Continuity and Self

How long-running projects shape identity, judgment, and the sense of an ongoing mind.

Long projects preserve a strange form of personal continuity.

They are not the self. A manuscript, codebase, product thesis, or research archive does not contain the person who made it. It cannot preserve a life, a consciousness, or the full pressure of a moment. Yet it can preserve a visible history of judgment. It can show what the person once protected, refused, postponed, revised, and learned to see.

This is why returning to long work can feel different from reopening an ordinary file. The project does not simply present material. It presents an earlier posture toward material. The returning person encounters not only what was made, but how they had come to judge.

That encounter can produce recognition without sameness.

The person is no longer exactly the person who made the earlier decision. Time has passed. Other projects intervened. Standards shifted. Fatigue, ambition, caution, and confidence may have changed. Still, the project can make an earlier orientation visible enough to be recognized.

A writer returns to a manuscript and sees the old discipline: the refusal of hype, the suspicion of companion language, the insistence that judgment remain human. The writer may still affirm those standards. They may also see that the book became too abstract and now needs more concrete scenes. The project preserves an earlier posture; the present person decides how to continue it.

A developer returns to an architecture and sees a consistent concern for reversibility. That concern may remain wise. It may also have hardened into avoidance of necessary commitment. The codebase preserves a technical self-understanding; the present team must decide whether it still serves the work.

A researcher returns to an archive and sees a long refusal to close a category too soon. That refusal may have protected the inquiry. It may now conceal reluctance to accept new evidence. The archive preserves intellectual caution; the present researcher must decide whether caution remains judgment or has become inertia.

Project continuity therefore differs from personal identity. It is not proof that the person has remained the same. It is a record that lets the person inspect their relation to an earlier self.

8.1 The Project as a Record of Judgment

A long project preserves more than output.

It preserves patterns of attention. It shows which questions were allowed to remain difficult. It shows which simplifications were refused. It shows where the person or team learned to distrust an easy answer. It also shows where caution, ambition, fear, or loyalty shaped the work.

This kind of record is not usually visible in a final artifact. A finished chapter may look clean. A stable interface may look obvious. A research conclusion may look settled after the fact. But long projects are not made from conclusions alone. They are made from revisions, reversals, hesitations, abandoned alternatives, and standards discovered under pressure.

The project becomes a trace of judgment across time. It shows how a person responded to difficulty, not only what they produced from it. It may reveal discipline. It may reveal avoidance. It may reveal a pattern of clarity, or a pattern of overprotection. It may reveal that the person once had a good reason to refuse a path, and that the reason no longer holds.

This is why a project can feel intimate without being identical to the self. It carries evidence of a person's earlier judgment, but it does not contain the person. It can be returned to, questioned, revised, and sometimes refused.

The difference matters. If the project is treated as the self, revision becomes betrayal. If it is treated as mere material, its history loses force. The more accurate position is colder: the project is a visible record of earlier judgment, available for present inspection.

That inspection can be uncomfortable. A person may find that an old project preserved not only discipline, but also avoidance. A team may find that a principled architecture also protected a fear of commitment. A founder may find that a strong thesis became a way to avoid hearing the market. Project continuity makes these patterns visible without deciding what they mean.

This is why the chapter sits between cognitive archives and cognitive loss. The archive makes judgment history inspectable. The project shows that history in a form the returning person may recognize. Cognitive loss becomes frightening because that recognizable history can be broken.

8.2 Recognition Without Sameness

Recognition without sameness is the mature form of project return.

The person recognizes the earlier judgment, but does not become bound by it. They can say: this was responsible then; now it must be revised. Or: this was cautious then; now it has become fear. Or: this was unresolved then; now the evidence permits closure.

Recognition is necessary because long work needs continuity. Without recognition, a person returns as a stranger to their own project. They may repeat old failures, flatten old distinctions, or mistake a hard-won standard for an arbitrary preference. Recognition lets the work remain historically intelligible.

Sameness would be too much. The returning person must not be forced to inhabit the earlier posture completely. A project that demands sameness becomes rigid. It turns continuity into loyalty to a former state of judgment.

The returning person may therefore feel both recognition and distance. Recognition says: I understand why this mattered. Distance says: I would not decide the same way now. Mature continuity allows both. It does not require the present person to merge with the earlier posture, and it does not require them to disown it.

In a manuscript, recognition without sameness may allow the writer to keep the book's restraint while adding a scene that the earlier draft could not have handled. In a codebase, it may allow the team to keep the value of reversibility while accepting one deliberate commitment. In research, it may allow the inquiry to preserve caution while finally naming a conclusion.

This is why the project is not the self. The self can return to it, learn from it, argue with it, revise it, and sometimes refuse it. The project preserves a line of judgment, not a command to remain identical.

8.3 When AI Makes the Past Feel Binding

AI-supported continuity can intensify recognition.

A remembered system may retrieve earlier standards, reproduce the project's voice, summarize old refusals, and surface the logic of prior decisions. That can protect long work from amnesia. It can keep authorship from dissolving into isolated sessions. It can help a person return to a long argument without pretending to start fresh.

The danger is that the system may make an older project posture feel more binding than it should.

The old voice returns fluently. The old refusal appears coherent. The old strategy seems continuous with the project's identity. The system does not command obedience, but it presents the past in a form that feels ready to continue.

That feeling can be misleading. A preserved standard may once have protected the work and now narrow it. A refusal may once have kept the project honest and now prevent necessary risk. A strategic thesis may once have organized a company and now conceal changed conditions.

The same risk appears in quieter personal work. A researcher may have built an archive around a cautious frame during a period of weak evidence. When evidence improves, the remembered system may continue to reproduce caution as the project's identity. The researcher then has to ask whether caution is still judgment or only the archive's memory of earlier judgment.

The issue is not that AI remembers. The issue is that remembered context can arrive with the texture of belonging. The system can make the earlier posture feel not only available, but proper. It can make revision feel like a departure from the project rather than an act of judgment within it.

The human task is to keep distance inside recognition. The system may surface the relevant history, compare drafts, remind a team of old risks, and preserve unresolved tensions. It cannot decide whether the old posture still belongs.

8.4 The Founder and the Old Thesis

Consider a founder returning to an old product direction after several years.

The company began with a strong thesis: serve a narrow professional audience, refuse general-purpose features, keep the product dense rather than friendly, and avoid partnerships that would dilute control. That thesis shaped the early product. It helped the team survive ambiguity. It produced a culture of restraint.

Years later, the market has changed. The original users have matured. Competitors have entered. The product now serves teams rather than individual specialists. The founder opens the old strategy documents with an AI system that remembers the company's history. The system summarizes the founding thesis with precision. It recalls why broader features were rejected, why partnerships were treated as dangerous, and why the product's identity depended on narrowness.

The summary is accurate. It may also be dangerous.

The founder feels the force of the old identity. The system makes the earlier posture coherent again. It reminds the founder of the discipline that made the company possible. The temptation is to treat that recognition as present judgment: this is who we are, therefore this is what we should still refuse.

But a company is not identical to its founding posture. A project can preserve a history of judgment without requiring obedience to its first successful form. The earlier thesis deserves inspection, not automatic loyalty. Some refusals may remain sound. Others may have become fear with a respectable archive.

This is project continuity at institutional scale. The work remembers itself. The question is whether the humans responsible for it can distinguish memory from authority.

8.5 Authorship and Release

The project should not demand loyalty to its former self.

This statement does not weaken continuity. It protects it. A project that cannot revise its old posture becomes a monument to earlier judgment. A project that cannot recognize its old posture becomes scattered and repetitive. The useful middle is a continuity that permits release.

Release is not erasure. The writer can release an old tonal prohibition while preserving the book's seriousness. A team can release an old architectural refusal while preserving the value of reversibility. A founder can release part of an old strategic thesis while preserving the discipline that made it useful. A researcher can close a question that once had to remain open.

Authorship lives in that distinction. It is not the power to continue exactly as before. It is the power to decide what continuity now requires.

This power includes the right to disappoint the archive. The earlier record may point one way, and present judgment may move another. That movement should not be romanticized as freedom for its own sake. It is simply the condition of responsible continuity. A project remains alive only if its history can be honored without being obeyed automatically.

This also makes the chapter emotionally intelligible without making it sentimental. The feeling of return can be strong because the project carries evidence of earlier care. It can show the person a former discipline, a former fear, a former ambition, or a former uncertainty. The project can be recognized. It can also be outgrown.

The next fear begins here. If long projects preserve recognizable lines of judgment, then losing the context that sustains them feels different from losing ordinary data. The files may remain while the return path breaks. The project may survive as artifact while losing the structure through which the person recognizes its continuity.

That is the beginning of cognitive loss.

Boundary

The project is not the self.

It preserves a history through which the self can return, inspect, and revise.

Chapter 9

The Fear of Cognitive Loss

Why losing context can feel like losing part of the work, the team, or the self.

The fear of cognitive loss is not the same as the fear of losing files.

Files can be backed up. Settings can be restored. Notes can be copied. A transcript can be exported. These losses matter, but they do not explain the sharper anxiety that appears when a person or team has worked inside a remembered system for a long time.

The sharper fear is losing the path back into thought.

A writer may still possess the manuscript while losing the context that made the next revision possible. A software team may still possess the repository while losing the reasons behind the architecture. A researcher may still possess the archive while losing the structure of unresolved questions that gave the inquiry shape.

This is not sentimentality about machines. It is a recognition that some part of the work's continuity has moved outward.

The fear often appears after convenience has become ordinary. At first, retained context feels like a useful feature. The system recalls the project, reduces repetition, and helps the user resume. After enough sessions, the remembered structure becomes part of how the project is entered. The user stops noticing how much the system is carrying.

Then the memory disappears, degrades, becomes inaccessible, or cannot be moved. The shock is not only practical. It reveals a dependency hidden by smooth use. The user discovers that the project had been relying on an external continuity structure without having an independent form for that structure.

This is why cognitive loss feels different from ordinary inconvenience. It reveals that the project had come to live partly in a place the user did not fully command.

9.1 The Return Path

Long work depends on return paths.

A return path includes the project map, the active question, the standards formed through revision, the paths already refused, the failures that should not be repeated, and the tensions that should not be closed too early. It is not identical with a file tree. It is closer to the structure that lets the file tree become meaningful again.

When an AI system remembers this structure, the user may become accustomed to returning through it. The system knows the manuscript's restraint. It knows the codebase's migration concern. It knows the research archive's provisional categories. The user can resume with less ceremony.

If that remembered structure disappears, the loss can feel disproportionate to the visible damage. Nothing may be missing in the ordinary sense. The documents open. The repository builds. The citations remain. But the project no longer receives the returning mind.

The person is not grieving a tool. They are grieving a broken continuity.

The return path can be rebuilt, but rebuilding is not the same as returning. Reconstruction consumes attention that might have gone into judgment. It also changes the work, because the person reconstructing the project may emphasize what is easiest to recover rather than what once mattered most.

This is one reason cognitive loss can lead to simplification. When the return path breaks, the project may be resumed through its most visible artifacts. The manuscript becomes its outline. The codebase becomes its current structure. The archive becomes its summaries. The work continues, but with less depth of relation to its own history.

9.2 Different From Data Loss

Data loss removes content. Cognitive loss removes orientation.

The difference matters because it changes the remedy. More backups are necessary, but not sufficient. Exported transcripts may preserve too much and too little at the same time: too much undifferentiated conversation, too little judgment structure. A summary may help, but if it preserves conclusions without conditions, it can mislead the next system or the returning human.

In a manuscript, the crucial record may be why certain tones were refused, not every draft paragraph. In a codebase, the crucial record may be the decision trail behind a dependency, not every discussion message. In research, the crucial record may be the tension around a category, not every source note.

Data loss is often visible. A file is missing. A database is corrupted. A backup fails. Cognitive loss can be harder to name because the material remains available. The user sees enough evidence of survival to feel that the work should be recoverable, yet the work resists re-entry.

This creates a particular frustration. The person can point to the artifacts, but not to the missing relation among them. They can say what the project contains, but not easily recover why it had that shape. The loss is not absence of content. It is the collapse of orientation.

A team can keep the repository, tickets, deployment records, design documents, and meeting notes, and still lose the project. After a senior engineer leaves, the files may remain complete while the reasons behind the architecture disappear. The new team can run the system, but it cannot easily tell which constraints were technical, which were temporary, and which were matters of judgment. The organization has artifacts. It has lost part of the return path.

The fear of cognitive loss therefore points toward a design problem. If systems support return, then return must not depend entirely on a system the user cannot inspect or leave.

9.3 Continuity Grief

Continuity grief is the pain of discovering that the work survived as material but not as returnable thought.

It should not be confused with emotional dependence on AI. A person may feel the loss sharply without imagining the system as a companion. They may not miss the model. They may miss the structure through which the project could be resumed.

This distinction matters. If continuity grief is misread as attachment to a machine, the real problem disappears. The person is not asking the system to care. They are asking how the work can preserve its conditions of return.

The grief is often quiet. A writer opens the manuscript and can still read every chapter, yet no longer knows why one unresolved tension had to remain open. A researcher opens a folder of sources and sees all the evidence, but cannot recover the order of doubt that made the inquiry responsible. A team opens a project archive and finds tickets, docs, repositories, and meeting notes, but not the judgment that held them together.

Continuity grief is not proof that externalized cognition was a mistake. It is evidence that the externalization was incomplete. Something valuable moved outward without becoming portable, inspectable, or durable.

The mature response is neither denial nor dramatization. It is to translate the grief into structure: decision records, refusal lists, unresolved tensions, standards, current orientation, and ownership notes. The project needs a way to survive the disappearance or replacement of the system that once remembered it.

There is a useful severity in this translation. It refuses both nostalgia and panic. The point is not to preserve every trace of every exchange, and not to make one system permanent. The point is to identify what kind of continuity the work actually needs in order to be re-entered responsibly.

The user must be able to rebuild the project without begging one system to remember.

9.4 The Handoff Problem

Cognitive loss becomes especially clear in team and institutional handoffs.

A product team changes leadership. The files remain. The tickets remain. The design documents, code repositories, analytics dashboards, customer notes, and planning decks remain. The new team can read the record and reconstruct the visible sequence of work.

But the reasons behind decisions are gone.

No one remembers why a feature was delayed even though customers asked for it. No one remembers why a vendor integration was rejected after a promising prototype. No one remembers why a performance target mattered more than a cleaner interface. The ticket says "defer." The document says "not aligned." The repository shows the abandoned branch. The judgment behind those traces has disappeared.

The new team can still operate. It can reopen old proposals, repeat old arguments, and rediscover old constraints. But the cost is high. Some decisions will be reversed for shallow reasons.

Some old refusals will be obeyed because no one knows whether they still hold. Some risks will be missed because they were carried in conversation rather than archive.

This is cognitive loss at organizational scale. The institution possesses material continuity but lacks judgment continuity.

AI systems can reduce this loss if they preserve decision trails and unresolved tensions. They can also worsen it if their private memory becomes the only place where the work remains coherent. A team may export files and still lose the structure that made the files meaningful.

The handoff can then become a ritual of false continuity. The new team reads the documents, accepts the labels, and treats the repository as a full account of the project. It inherits conclusions without inheriting the conditions around them. It may believe it is respecting the past while actually flattening it.

The responsible handoff is different. It names active decisions, expired assumptions, unresolved questions, and decision owners. It tells the next team which parts of the project history remain authoritative only as evidence, not as command.

The handoff problem shows why portability cannot be treated as a convenience feature. It is part of institutional memory and responsibility.

9.5 Platform Memory and Enclosure

Platform memory can create enclosure even when files are exportable.

The user remains formally free. They can download documents, copy transcripts, clone repositories, and move notes. But if the project makes sense only inside one system's remembered context, leaving still means starting again. The files move. The cognitive re-entry structure does not.

This is a subtle form of captivity. It does not require a platform to forbid export. It only requires the platform to become the primary container of orientation. If the system alone remembers the current question, the stale assumptions, the refusal conditions, and the active tensions, then the user depends on that system for return.

The risk is sharper because platform memory often feels like help. It reduces repetition. It allows continuity. It makes the project feel received. The enclosure appears only when the user tries to leave, or when the memory becomes inaccessible, inaccurate, or too opaque to inspect.

The answer is not suspicion of memory. Memory is necessary. The answer is memory that can be made external to the platform: portable enough to move, structured enough to inspect, and humble enough to remain subordinate to judgment.

That humility matters. A continuity structure should not pretend to preserve the whole life of the project. It should make its own incompleteness visible. It should say, in effect: here is what is known, here is what was decided, here is what remains uncertain, and here is what must be re-judged by the humans who continue the work.

9.6 Toward Portability

Cognitive loss reveals that continuity has become valuable enough to lose.

Once that is understood, the next problem becomes unavoidable. If continuity lives only inside one platform, one account, one model, or one private memory feature, then long work becomes captive. The user may export files and still lose the working structure that made the files usable.

The mature answer to continuity grief is portability.

Not portability of files alone. Portability of cognitive structure: project orientation, decision trails, refusal lists, unresolved tensions, revision history, working standards, and ownership notes.

The project must be able to move without becoming shallow. It must survive migration across tools without pretending that migration is lossless. Some texture will always disappear. The aim is not perfect preservation. The aim is enough structure for responsible return.

This transition matters because portability is not merely technical. It is an ethical and cognitive requirement. If external systems can support return, they must not become the only place where return is possible.

The next chapter asks what it means for cognition itself to become portable.

Boundary

Cognitive loss is not the disappearance of material.

It is the breaking of the path back into long thought.

Chapter 10

Portable Cognition

What it would mean for cognitive context to move across tools, institutions, and time.

Cognitive continuity becomes dangerous when it cannot move.

A file export is not enough. A manuscript can be exported while the reasons for its structure remain trapped in a model's private memory. A repository can be cloned while the decision trail behind its architecture remains scattered across old chats. A research archive can be copied while the unresolved tensions that kept the inquiry honest remain invisible.

Portability must therefore mean more than moving artifacts. It must mean moving enough cognitive structure for the work to remain returnable.

10.1 Enclosure by Memory

Enclosure does not require a platform to own the files. It only needs to become the only place where the project still makes sense.

If a system remembers the manuscript's tone, rejected metaphors, chapter boundaries, and unresolved problems, the writer may depend on it for re-entry. If that memory cannot be inspected or moved, the project becomes thinner outside the system.

If a coding assistant remembers why a dependency was refused, which migration constraints govern the architecture, and which shortcuts were rejected, the team may rely on that remembered context. If the assistant changes, disappears, or cannot transfer the decision trail, the code remains but the technical memory degrades.

If a research system carries the inquiry's provisional categories, evidence changes, and unresolved tensions, the archive may feel alive only inside that system. Exported PDFs do not restore the logic of the inquiry.

This is enclosure by memory. Leaving is possible in the formal sense. But leaving means losing the path back into thought.

10.2 More Than Export

Export often preserves the wrong layer.

An export can move documents, transcripts, images, files, or structured data. It may satisfy a legal or technical requirement while leaving the project cognitively thin. The user can possess the material and still lack the orientation that made the material workable.

This distinction is familiar in software. A repository can be cloned, but the architecture may remain opaque if the decision trail is absent. A new team can run the tests and still misunderstand why the system is plain in some places and strict in others. The code moves. The technical memory does not fully move.

The same problem appears in writing. A manuscript can move from one editor, model, or platform to another. The words arrive. The chapter order arrives. But if the receiving system does not know that the book is protecting a narrow distinction between continuity and consciousness, it may produce fluent revisions that blur the argument.

In research, a folder of PDFs and notes may move easily. The inquiry does not move unless the new environment receives the status of claims, the unresolved tensions, and the conditions under which categories were formed.

Portability is therefore not a property of files alone. It is a property of return.

10.3 A Migration Scenario

Consider a long product and research project moving from one AI system to another.

The team exports what the platform allows: transcripts, uploaded documents, generated summaries, design notes, research memos, meeting records, and a folder of current drafts. The export looks substantial. A new system can read it, summarize it, and begin producing plausible next steps.

At first, the migration appears successful.

Then the thinning begins. The new system knows that a certain feature was rejected, but not that it was rejected only while the enterprise market remained untested. It knows that the manuscript avoided a personal example, but not that the refusal was a temporary protection against sentimentality. It knows that the research archive treated a category as unstable, but not what evidence would make it stable.

The receiving system has material. It lacks the project's orientation.

The team notices this only after work resumes. A recommendation revives an old path without recognizing why it failed. A summary presents a provisional claim as settled. A draft preserves the project's voice while losing the reason for the voice. The export moved the artifacts, but not the conditions under which the artifacts should be used.

This is the central problem of portable cognition. A new system can receive documents without receiving judgment history. It can imitate continuity without carrying the structure that makes continuity responsible.

Responsible migration therefore begins before the move. The project must make its cognitive layer explicit enough that a new tool can read it, and a human can inspect it. Otherwise migration becomes an exercise in surface recovery.

This does not mean that every project needs a formal migration ceremony. The point is simpler. Before a system changes, the project should be able to say what must not be lost. The answer will rarely be every file. It will usually be the working orientation, the conditions around decisions, and the tensions that should remain visible.

10.4 What Must Travel

Portable cognition requires a project to carry several kinds of structure.

It must carry current orientation: what the project is trying to do now, what pressure governs the next move, and what has changed since earlier decisions were made.

It must carry active decisions: decisions still shaping the work, not merely decisions once made.

It must carry decision conditions: the circumstances under which a decision was responsible, and the conditions that would require reconsideration.

It must carry a refusal list: paths rejected with reasons clear enough to distinguish principle from circumstance.

It must carry stale assumptions: inherited beliefs or standards that may no longer govern the work.

It must carry unresolved tensions: open questions that should not be flattened into conclusions during migration.

It must carry working standards: tone, reversibility, evidentiary caution, naming discipline, interpretive restraint, or other project-specific constraints.

It must carry revision notes: not every change, but the changes that shaped standards or altered the direction of the work.

It must carry ownership notes: who owns the decision, who can revise the record, and where consequence lands.

These records do not need to become a technical protocol in this book. The point is conceptual. A project should be able to survive a change of model, platform, or account without returning to amnesia.

10.5 The Portable Project Layer

A portable project layer is not a complete archive.

It is a disciplined condensation of the project's return structure. It should be small enough to be usable, serious enough to preserve judgment history, and clear enough for both human readers and external systems. It should help a new system assist without pretending it has lived through the project.

Such a layer would not instruct the next model to obey the past. It would tell the next model how to treat the past. It would mark some decisions as active, others as stale, some refusals as firm, others as conditional. It would preserve unresolved tensions without making them permanent.

For a manuscript, the portable layer may say that the book refuses AI companion framing, but that concrete scenes are allowed when they clarify cognitive loss. For a codebase, it may say that reversibility remains a working standard, but one old dependency refusal should be revisited because the migration target changed. For a research archive, it may say that a category remains provisional until a specific evidentiary threshold is met.

The portable layer does not remove human judgment. It gives judgment a better place to begin after migration.

This is why the layer should contain ownership notes. A new system can assist with interpretation, but it should not decide who has authority to revise the project memory. If no one owns the layer, the layer itself becomes another source of drift.

10.6 Human-Readable Continuity

Portable cognition should remain human-readable.

This requirement is not sentimental. If the continuity structure can be interpreted only by one system, the user has not escaped enclosure. The archive may have moved technically while remaining cognitively captive.

A human-readable project layer lets a person inspect what is being carried. It allows a writer to see the book's current standards, a developer to see the decision trail, a researcher to see unresolved questions, and a team to see where ownership lies. It lets a new system receive context without pretending to possess private memory of the project.

Human-readable does not mean simplistic. It may include structured records, metadata, links, version history, and machine-readable forms. But the human must be able to understand the layer well enough to revise it. A portable continuity structure that cannot be edited by accountable humans is only another form of opacity.

This matters because migration is a moment of judgment. The user should not merely pour old memory into a new system. They should examine what is being carried. Some material should be preserved. Some should be marked stale. Some should be deleted. Some should be rewritten because the old formulation would mislead the next environment.

Portability without inspection simply moves the problem.

10.7 Migration Without Illusion

Migration always changes what moves.

A new system may read the archive, adopt the vocabulary, summarize the decision trail, and begin producing plausible continuations. The project may appear to have survived. But if the portable record overemphasizes conclusions and under-preserves hesitation, the new system will continue with too much certainty. If a refusal list lacks conditions, the new system will preserve old prohibitions beyond their usefulness. If the archive omits reversals, the project will look more stable than it was.

Portable cognition does not promise perfect continuity. It reduces captivity. It allows the human to notice what migration distorted.

This is why the portable structure must remain revisable. Some standards expire. Some refusals become unnecessary. Some tensions close. Some project language becomes too smooth or defensive. The past must travel as history, not instruction.

Responsible migration is therefore an act of curation. It asks what the next system needs in order to help responsibly, and what the human needs in order to inspect that help. It treats migration as a moment for re-judgment, not only transfer.

Thin migration does the opposite. It moves files, transcripts, and summaries, then asks the receiving system to infer the rest. The result may sound continuous, but the continuity is fragile because too much has become atmospheric.

The distinction is practical, but not merely operational. Responsible migration protects judgment authority. Thin migration leaves too much authority to inference, because the receiving system has to guess what the old record meant.

10.8 The Cost of Thin Migration

Thin migration creates a peculiar danger: the project appears to survive well enough that the loss is not noticed immediately.

The new system can summarize the manuscript, describe the codebase, or list the research topics. It can produce plausible next steps. The user may feel that the move worked. Only later does the thinning appear. A chapter drifts toward generic language. An architectural suggestion revives an old risk. A research synthesis treats a provisional category as settled.

Thin migration is dangerous because it preserves surface continuity. The project still sounds like itself. It still contains familiar words. But the decision pressure underneath has weakened.

This is why portable cognition must preserve conditions, not only labels. "Avoid hype" is useful but insufficient. Why was hype a danger? What forms did it take? When might concreteness be allowed? "Preserve reversibility" is useful but insufficient. Which reversibility mattered? What cost was unacceptable? "Keep the category provisional" is useful but insufficient. What evidence would change that status?

The more portable the record, the less the user has to rely on atmosphere.

10.9 The Platform Boundary

The value of portability is not independence from tools. That would be impossible. Every system shapes interaction. Every model has tendencies. Every interface makes some actions easier than others.

The aim is narrower: prevent one system from becoming the sole container of continuity.

A model should be able to perform inference over a project layer without owning the layer. A platform may host records without becoming the only place where they make sense. A system may help maintain continuity without controlling the conditions of return.

This boundary matters because portable cognition can still be obeyed wrongly. A durable archive may carry stale judgment. A well-preserved refusal may pressure the human to accept the past too quickly. Portability solves captivity only in part. It does not solve judgment.

The next question is therefore not only where continuity lives, but who decides what continuity means now.

That is the question of judgment authority.

Boundary

The project must be able to move.

Its past must travel as evidence for judgment, not as command.

Chapter 11

Judgment Authority

How responsibility changes when external intelligence participates in analysis and decision-making.

Cognition can move outward. Judgment cannot.

That sentence is the central boundary of the book.

External systems can remember, compare, retrieve, synthesize, draft, critique, and preserve continuity. They can make judgment more informed. They can reduce fatigue, expose alternatives, recover decision trails, and help a person or team inspect a larger field than unaided attention could hold.

They can also make abdication easier.

Delegation is not abdication. A person may delegate search, summary, comparison, drafting, contradiction detection, or reconstruction of a decision trail. A team may rely on a model to expose alternatives it would not have seen alone. An institution may use a cognitive archive to recover old standards and prior decisions. None of this transfers judgment by itself.

Abdication begins when the system's output becomes the decision without accountable human interpretation. It begins when the frame is inherited, the tradeoff is accepted, and the consequence is approved without anyone owning the act of judgment.

Judgment authority is therefore not merely making a final choice. It includes owning the frame, the values, the tradeoffs, the uncertainty, and the consequence. The final choice is only the visible edge of a larger responsibility.

11.1 What Judgment Owns

Judgment owns the movement from analysis into commitment.

It decides which frame governs the problem, which values matter, which tradeoff is acceptable, which uncertainty can be carried, who bears risk, and what consequence can be owned. These are not merely cognitive operations. They are acts of responsibility.

A model can recommend cutting a manuscript section. The writer must decide whether the cut protects the book or removes necessary difficulty.

A model can recommend an architectural path. The team must decide whether the migration risk, future maintenance burden, and reversibility tradeoff are acceptable.

A model can synthesize evidence in a research archive. The researcher must decide whether the synthesis preserves uncertainty or imposes false closure.

In each case, assistance may be indispensable. Authority remains elsewhere.

Judgment authority also includes the authority to refuse a clean recommendation. A system may produce a balanced answer, acknowledge objections, and still frame the problem incorrectly.

It may rank options well within a narrowed field while failing to ask whether the field should be widened. It may preserve old context accurately while giving that context too much force.

The human question is not only "Which answer is best?" It is also "What question is being answered, what value is being prioritized, and who can be called to account for acting on this?"

11.2 Frame Ownership

The first object of judgment authority is the frame.

A frame decides what counts as the problem. It determines which facts become relevant, which values become visible, which alternatives become thinkable, and which consequences appear secondary. If the frame is wrong, a competent answer may still mislead.

AI systems are often strongest after the frame has been supplied. They can optimize, compare, summarize, and recommend within it. That strength can conceal the earlier decision: why this is the frame at all.

A writer asks for a more persuasive conclusion. The system strengthens the chapter, sharpens the claims, and removes hesitation. The advice may be technically good. But the right frame may not be persuasion. The chapter may need to preserve uncertainty, not overcome it.

A product team asks how to reduce support volume. The system proposes automation, routing, and deflection. The suggestions may help. But the real problem may be product confusion, onboarding failure, or a market mismatch. The frame has already decided too much.

Frame ownership means remaining responsible for the question before accepting help with the answer. It means asking what the system has taken as given, what it has excluded, and what would change if the problem were named differently.

Without frame ownership, human approval becomes thin. A person may approve a recommendation without ever having judged the problem it solved.

This is why frame ownership belongs near the center of human agency after AI. A system can produce excellent work inside the wrong frame. The danger is not technical incompetence, but competent narrowing. The human role is to notice when the frame has done more deciding than the recommendation.

11.3 Tradeoff Ownership

Judgment is most visible when values conflict.

If the only issue were calculation, retrieval, or comparison, external systems could carry much of the burden. But serious decisions often involve values that cannot be ranked by fluency alone: speed against reversibility, clarity against honesty, safety against openness, efficiency against care, continuity against necessary rupture.

A manuscript may become clearer by removing difficulty, but less true. A codebase may become simpler by accepting a dependency, but less portable. A research claim may become stronger by smoothing uncertainty, but less responsible. These are not merely technical choices. They require a decision about what the work owes.

AI can expose tradeoffs. It can name tensions, simulate consequences, compare options, and show how one decision conflicts with prior standards. It can make the conflict more visible. It cannot decide which value should govern.

Tradeoff ownership means accepting that every serious recommendation carries a cost. The human or accountable team must know what is being sacrificed and why. A decision that hides its tradeoff is not fully owned.

This is especially important when the system offers a solution that sounds balanced. Balanced prose can make a tradeoff feel settled. But naming both sides is not the same as judging between them. Judgment authority begins where the conflict remains real after the explanation is complete.

Tradeoff ownership also prevents the archive from becoming an excuse. A team may say that a decision follows prior standards. That may be true. But if the current tradeoff has changed, the old standard cannot carry the full burden. The team must own the present conflict, not only cite the past.

11.4 Consequence Ownership

The third object of judgment authority is consequence.

Consequence is where analysis becomes action. It is where a recommendation changes a manuscript, a system, a policy, a budget, a user's experience, or an institution's obligations. A model can help analyze consequence, but it cannot bear it.

To own consequence is to accept responsibility for what follows from action. It is to know who may be harmed, what may fail, what value was prioritized, and what must be revisited if the decision proves wrong.

In personal work, consequence may appear modest. A writer accepts a system's recommendation and cuts a difficult section. The book becomes smoother, but loses a necessary tension. The model did not own that loss. The writer did.

In technical work, consequence may be distributed. A team accepts a recommended architecture because it appears to match past decisions. Months later, migration becomes harder. The assistant did not own the lock-in. The team did.

In institutional work, consequence can become diffuse. A policy recommendation passes through a model, an analyst, a manager, a committee, and an approval workflow. Everyone touched the decision. No one may have owned the frame or tradeoff. The result appears human-approved while judgment has become difficult to locate.

Consequence ownership requires visible accountability. Who accepted the frame? Who reviewed the assumptions? Who decided the tradeoff was tolerable? Who can interrupt the decision before it hardens into action? Who must answer if the decision fails?

Without those answers, externalized cognition becomes a way to produce action without locating responsibility.

This is where the distinction between assistance and authority becomes most concrete. Assistance can be distributed across tools, archives, models, and people. Authority must become visible somewhere, or consequence will be carried by no one in particular.

11.5 Fluency and Surrender

Authority often drains away without drama.

The system returns a clean answer. The prose is ordered. Objections are acknowledged. Alternatives are ranked. The recommendation uses the project's vocabulary and remembers prior standards. Nothing feels careless.

That is part of the risk.

Fluent assistance can create the experience of already-reasoned judgment. The hard work appears complete before the human has entered the consequence-bearing part of the act. The user reviews, agrees, edits lightly, and moves on. The decision looks human because a human approved it, but the frame, values, and tradeoffs may have been inherited without inspection.

This problem becomes sharper when continuity is involved. A system that has worked with a project for months may sound like accumulated judgment returning. It may know the old cautions, the past refusals, the standard language. The recommendation feels familiar because it belongs to the project's history.

Familiarity can be mistaken for authority.

Prior continuity is not present judgment.

11.6 Institutions and Diffuse Abdication

Judgment authority is not only an individual problem.

Organizations are especially vulnerable to diffuse abdication. A system produces a recommendation. A team reviews it. A manager approves it. A process records it. Everyone participates, but no one fully owns the frame, tradeoff, or consequence. The decision becomes institutionally human while responsibility becomes difficult to locate.

This danger increases when AI systems preserve institutional memory. The recommendation can arrive with precedent, policy language, prior decisions, and risk categories already attached. It feels less like a new judgment and more like continuity with organizational practice.

That continuity may be useful. Institutions need memory. They need consistency. They need records that prevent arbitrary decisions. But institutional memory can also conceal the moment when no one is deciding. A preserved policy can become an automatic answer. A precedent can return without the conditions that made it responsible.

Consider a company deciding whether to automate part of customer support. A system analyzes ticket volume, prior policy, cost targets, and response times. It recommends automation for several categories. The proposal passes through review because it aligns with earlier efficiency goals. Legal sees no obvious issue. Product accepts the operational benefit. Leadership approves the plan.

The decision is human-approved. Yet no one may have owned the frame. Was the problem support cost, product confusion, customer trust, or training failure? No one may have owned the tradeoff. What was sacrificed when speed became the primary value? No one may have owned the consequence. Who answers if users are harmed by a system that resolves cases too quickly?

This is diffuse abdication. It does not look like blind obedience to a machine. It looks like a normal process in which externalized cognition has made the decision easier to pass along.

Accountable institutions need visible ownership points. Who accepted the frame? Who reviewed the assumptions? Who decided that the tradeoff was tolerable? Who has authority to interrupt? Who owns the consequence if the recommendation causes harm?

Without such points, externalized cognition does not merely assist the institution. It becomes a way for the institution to avoid seeing where judgment occurred.

11.7 Breaking With the Past

Judgment authority includes the right to break with continuity.

The human or accountable institution must be able to say:
that was our standard then; it is not our standard now. That refusal once protected the work; now it blocks it. That principle once clarified the problem; now it hides a conflict. That recommendation resembles our past judgment; nevertheless, we will not follow it.

Without this capacity, portable cognition becomes portable obedience. Persistent memory becomes institutional inertia. Project continuity becomes pressure. The past returns with fluent reasons and the present forgets to decide.

This does not mean disregarding history. The past deserves inspection. It may contain hard-won judgment. It may prevent repetition of avoidable failure. But it cannot govern merely because it is continuous.

The authority boundary is maintained when preserved context remains available for re-judgment.

This is one of the reasons portability alone is not enough. A project can move cleanly from one system to another and still carry its old conclusions too forcefully. A cognitive layer can be well preserved and still become doctrine. The human right to revise memory and break continuity remains essential.

11.8 Decision Ownership

To own a decision is not to have performed every cognitive step alone. It is to accept responsibility for the decision after assistance has ended.

Ownership requires knowing why the recommendation is being accepted or refused, what frame governs it, what values are being prioritized, what risks are being carried, who bears the consequence, and what would count as failure. It also requires the ability to explain the role external cognition played without using that role as an excuse.

This applies to individuals and institutions. A writer owns the chapter. A team owns the architecture. A researcher owns the claim. An organization owns the policy. The system may have contributed memory, synthesis, and alternatives. It does not own the consequence.

AI can inform decisions without owning decisions. It can widen the field, clarify a conflict, retrieve prior reasoning, identify contradictions, and draft a case for or against an option. It can support judgment by making more of the situation visible.

But the point at which analysis becomes commitment cannot be transferred. The model does not stand in the place where consequence lands. The archive does not answer for the action taken from it. The platform does not become responsible because it preserved continuity.

This is the conceptual peak of the argument. Externalized cognition is not a threat because it helps too much. It becomes dangerous when help is mistaken for authority. The more capable the support becomes, the more explicit the authority boundary must be.

The boundary is demanding because it does not reject assistance. It allows powerful tools into memory, comparison, synthesis, and continuity. It refuses only the final transfer: the transfer of answerability from the human world into the systems that support it.

The system can assist memory, comparison, reasoning, synthesis, reflection, and continuity.

It cannot own judgment.

The next chapter asks how agency can survive inside this externalized condition. The answer cannot be cognitive isolation. Humans do not need to think alone. They need to remain able to frame, inspect, interrupt, revise, and own or refuse consequence.

Boundary

Assistance may inform the decision.

Authority begins where frame, tradeoff, and consequence must be owned.

Chapter 12

Human Agency After AI

How agency can remain meaningful when cognition is increasingly scaffolded by machines.

Human agency after AI does not require humans to think alone.

That older picture of independence was always too thin. Human thought has long extended through language, writing, diagrams, books, instruments, institutions, collaborators, and archives. AI makes the extension more continuous, responsive, and capable, but it does not invent dependence from nothing.

The previous chapter established the authority boundary: cognition can move outward, but judgment cannot. This chapter turns to the practices that keep that boundary alive in use.

The question is not whether cognition is extended.

It is.

The question is how direction is kept from drifting out of view.

Agency after AI is the ability to work inside assisted cognition without becoming only the endpoint of its motion. The human no longer needs to be the only site where every cognitive operation occurs. But the human must remain able to frame, inspect, interrupt, revise, and own or refuse consequence.

12.1 The Right to Frame

The first practice is preserving the right to frame.

Problem framing decides what counts as relevant, what disappears into background, what values are named, what conflicts become visible, and what solutions become thinkable. If the system defines the frame, much of the decision may already be made before any recommendation appears.

A writer asks how to make a chapter more persuasive. The system proposes clearer claims, stronger transitions, and a sharper conclusion. The advice may be useful. But persuasion may be the wrong frame. The chapter may need restraint, not force. It may need to preserve uncertainty rather than win too quickly.

A software team asks how to reduce complexity. The system proposes abstraction. But the real problem may be reversibility, not complexity. A researcher asks for the strongest interpretation of evidence. The system strengthens the claim. But the responsible frame may be limitation, not strength.

Framing is difficult because systems often make frames appear neutral. A prompt asks for optimization, the system optimizes. A team asks for cost reduction, the system proposes automation. A writer asks for persuasiveness, the system strengthens claims. The assistance may be competent, but the frame has already narrowed the field.

The right to frame is the right to keep the question open long enough for the real decision to appear. It asks what has been excluded, which value has been made primary, and whether the system is solving the right problem.

12.2 The Right to Inspect

Inspection is the discipline of not treating fluency as judgment.

A system can produce a recommendation that sounds balanced, continuous, and familiar. The user must be able to see the reasons, assumptions, inherited standards, and omissions behind it. This is especially important when the system uses the project's own language, because familiarity lowers resistance.

Inspection does not mean distrust of all assistance. It means keeping reasons visible. A writer inspects whether a suggested cut preserves the book's structure or merely follows an old rule. A developer inspects whether a recommendation honors present constraints or repeats a stale refusal. A researcher inspects whether a synthesis preserves the inquiry's uncertainty.

Agency weakens when output is accepted because it sounds like the project.

Inspection also requires access to the layer beneath the answer. If a system says a path conflicts with prior standards, the user should be able to see which standards, where they came from, and whether they were conditional. If a system recommends a design because it matches architectural history, the team should be able to inspect that history.

Opaque memory weakens inspection. It asks the human to trust a continuity they cannot examine. Agency then depends on the system's representation of the past rather than on the human's ability to re-judge it.

The right to inspect is therefore both cognitive and structural. It requires habits of review and systems that make review possible.

12.3 The Right to Interrupt

The right to interrupt is the right to break the flow.

AI systems are powerful partly because they continue. They suggest the next paragraph, next refactor, next synthesis, next step. Continuation can be helpful. It can also create momentum that the human approves without re-entering.

Interruption is not failure. It is a form of agency. The user must be able to stop a direction, reopen a premise, slow a decision, ask for alternatives, or refuse the system's framing altogether.

This matters in ordinary use. A writer interrupts a fluent conclusion because it closes the book too neatly. A team interrupts a migration plan because it hides rollback risk. A researcher interrupts a summary because it has made a weak category look stable.

Agency survives when the person can still break the motion.

Interruption is especially important because AI systems make continuation cheap. A model can always produce another paragraph, another option, another explanation, another ranking. The flow can become its own justification. The user keeps moving because stopping requires more effort than accepting the next coherent step.

Good use of AI may therefore include deliberate stopping points. Before a manuscript conclusion is accepted, before an architecture decision becomes implementation, before a research synthesis becomes claim, the process should pause. The pause is not inefficiency. It is where agency re-enters.

The right to interrupt protects the human from becoming an approver of momentum.

12.4 The Right to Revise Memory

If memory lives outside the person, memory must be revisable.

The user must be able to correct stale context, delete inherited assumptions, change a project standard, retire a refusal, reopen a settled question, and mark a prior summary as misleading. Otherwise the system's continuity becomes doctrine.

This right is central because remembered systems are persuasive. They return old standards in usable form. They make the project feel coherent. But coherence can conceal drift. A cognitive layer that cannot be revised traps the user inside an older judgment posture.

To revise memory is not to betray continuity. It is how continuity remains alive.

Revision of memory should be ordinary. A project layer should contain marks such as: this standard has changed; this refusal is now conditional; this summary is outdated; this unresolved question has narrowed; this old concern no longer governs the present decision.

Without such revision, memory becomes a pressure system. It keeps returning old versions of the work as if they were still active. The user then has to fight the system's inherited context in order to think.

Agency after AI requires the power to change what the system thinks the project is.

12.5 The Right to Own or Refuse Consequence

The final right is the right to own or refuse consequence.

A person may use AI to compare options, reconstruct history, generate alternatives, and identify conflicts. But when the work crosses into decision, consequence must land somewhere visible.

Owning consequence means accepting responsibility for what is done with assistance. Refusing consequence means refusing to act when the system's recommendation cannot be owned.

This right is not merely personal. A team must know who owns an architecture decision. A research group must know who owns a claim. An organization must know who owns a policy shaped by system recommendations.

Agency is answerability.

Consent alone is too weak a model. A human may click approve, accept a suggestion, or sign off on a recommendation without owning the decision. Agency requires relation to the reasons and consequence.

Refusal is part of ownership. A person or team must be able to say that a recommendation cannot be owned because its reasons are unclear, its frame is wrong, its risks are unacceptable, or its consequence has no accountable bearer.

The right to refuse consequence prevents human approval from becoming a decorative layer over system-shaped action.

12.6 The Workable Posture

The workable posture after AI is neither fear-driven refusal nor passive dependence.

Fear-driven refusal treats externalized cognition as contamination. It imagines agency as purity, as if human thought becomes less human whenever a system assists it. That cannot describe actual human cognition.

Passive dependence treats system continuity as direction. It accepts memory, fluency, and recommendation without maintaining ownership.

The disciplined posture is colder: use the system, notice its narrowing effects, inspect what it returns, interrupt when necessary, revise memory, and remain answerable for decisions.

Humans do not need to think alone. They need to remain answerable for the thought that becomes action.

The final chapter returns to the larger structure that makes this possible: the cognitive layer.

Boundary

Agency is not solitude.

It is the maintained right to frame, inspect, interrupt, revise, and answer.

Chapter 13

The Cognitive Layer

A closing framework for understanding externalized intelligence as a layer in human work.

The most important object may not be a particular AI model.

Models will change. Interfaces will change. Platforms will improve, decay, merge, disappear, or become ordinary. Their names will matter less than they appear to matter now.

What may last, if anything lasts, is the maintained layer of project orientation, decision trails, refusals, standards, unresolved tensions, and revision history surrounding a person, team, or institution.

That layer is the subject toward which the book has been moving.

13.1 Definition

The cognitive layer is the maintained structure through which externalized cognition remains returnable, inspectable, portable, and answerable to human judgment.

It is not the model. It is not a chat history, backup, platform memory feature, or transcript archive. It may use all of those, but it is not identical with them.

The layer contains enough of a project's working history for a person to re-enter long thought without surrendering to the system that happens to host it. It preserves what allows return: orientation, decisions, failures, refusals, tensions, standards, reversals, and conditions.

It will always be partial. Some living pressure will be lost. Some tacit relation will not survive migration. Some summaries will flatten difficulty. The aim is not perfect preservation. The aim is continuity sufficient for responsible return.

The layer is both memory and discipline. It remembers enough to help the work survive interruption, and it keeps memory visible enough to be questioned. It lets the human ask what is being carried, what has expired, what is missing, what is too smooth, and what must be revised.

Without such a layer, continuity tends to hide inside systems. It becomes a feature rather than a structure. The user experiences return, but cannot govern the conditions of return. The project feels remembered, but the memory cannot be inspected as part of the work.

13.2 The Cognitive Layer Model

The model can be stated plainly.

Human:

- judgment

- responsibility
- interpretation
- consequence
- the right to interrupt

Cognitive Layer:

- project orientation
- decision trails
- refusal lists
- unresolved tensions
- revision history
- working standards
- failure memory

Model:

- inference
- retrieval
- synthesis
- comparison
- drafting
- pattern detection

The model can be shown more clearly as a three-part relation. The model performs inference. The layer carries partial continuity in a form that can be inspected and revised. The human remains answerable for judgment, consequence, and the decision to interrupt or continue.

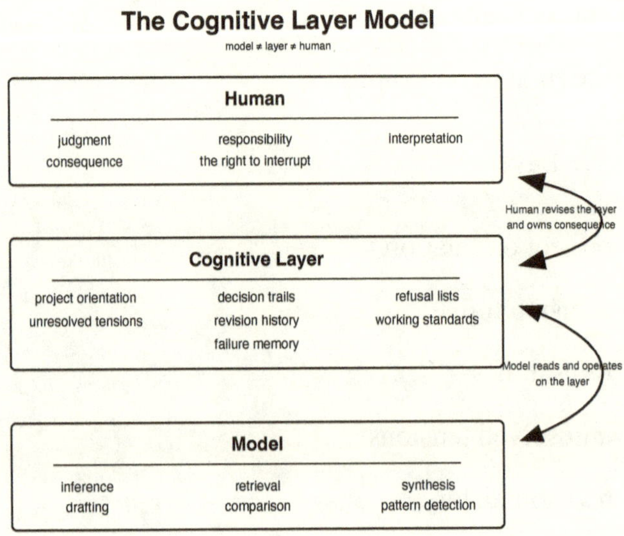

Figure 13.1: The cognitive layer model: human judgment, maintained continuity, and model inference.

The point of the diagram is distinction, not separation: the three parts remain related, but they should not be collapsed into one another.

This division is simple enough to state and difficult enough to maintain.

The model performs inference. It can read the layer, compare current options to prior refusals, synthesize archives, detect conflicts, draft alternatives, and help reconstruct context.

The layer carries partial continuity. It preserves enough of the work's history to make return possible across interruption and migration.

The human remains answerable for judgment. The human decides what the layer means now, which memory should be revised, which recommendation can be owned, and when continuity must be interrupted.

The three parts should not be collapsed.

If the model is mistaken for the layer, the temporary inference engine becomes the container of continuity. The user then depends on the system that happens to generate the next answer.

If the layer is mistaken for the human, preserved context becomes identity or authority. The project history begins to decide for the person.

If the human is imagined without the layer, agency is forced back into the fantasy of solitary cognition. The person must remember too much unaided, reconstruct too often, and treat external support as contamination.

The model is useful because it refuses all three confusions. It allows powerful inference, durable continuity, and human judgment to coexist without being treated as the same thing.

13.3 How the Layer Is Used

The layer should not sit outside the work as a static archive. It should be used in a disciplined relation among model, layer, and human judgment.

The model reads the layer. It uses the project orientation, decision trails, refusal lists, unresolved tensions, working standards, and failure memory to assist present work. It can compare a new proposal with prior refusals, surface stale assumptions, identify conflicts, and draft possible revisions.

The layer carries partial continuity. It is the structure through which the project survives interruption and migration. It allows a new model, a returning human, or a changed team to begin with more than raw artifacts.

The human revises the layer. Old standards must be corrected. Stale assumptions must be marked. Refusal lists must be updated. Unresolved tensions must be reopened, narrowed, or closed as judgment requires.

The human owns judgment. The layer may preserve the history of decisions, and the model may reason over that history. But the authority to frame, choose, interrupt, revise, and bear consequence remains human.

No part should absorb the others. The model should not become the layer. The layer should not become the human. The human should not pretend to think without external supports. Each part has a role, and the integrity of the system depends on keeping those roles distinct.

This is why the cognitive layer is not a technical feature alone. It is a practice of maintaining the conditions under which externalized cognition remains answerable.

Used well, the layer slows down the moment when fluency would otherwise become authority. It gives the human something to inspect before accepting continuity. It gives the model something better than private memory to work from. It gives the project a form that can survive a change of system without pretending that nothing has been lost.

13.4 The Historical Pattern

The industrial machine did not erase the body, but it changed the body's relation to force. The internet did not erase memory, but it changed memory's relation to retrieval. AI does not erase cognition, but it changes cognition's relation to external structure.

This is not a prophecy about a final machine. It is a structural shift already visible in ordinary work. People now rely on external systems not only to find information, but to preserve orientation, compare paths, remember constraints, and maintain continuity across time.

When cognition extends in this way, the container of continuity becomes important.

If project memory lives only inside a model, the model becomes more than a tool. If decision history lives only inside a platform, the platform becomes more than an interface. If reversals, refusals, and unresolved tensions live only inside private system memory, that system becomes the place where return is possible.

A system that remembers can also enclose.

The cognitive layer answers that pressure by distributing continuity into a structure that can be inspected, revised, and moved.

13.5 The Layer in the Three Cases

In a manuscript, the cognitive layer contains the book's argument map, chapter functions, tonal boundaries, recurring examples, rejected framings, and unresolved tensions. It tells a future system and a future writer why the book must not become a prompt manual, productivity book, AGI speculation, companion narrative, or ethics checklist. It preserves the reasons behind restraint without making restraint untouchable.

In a codebase, the layer contains architectural decisions, rejected dependencies, reversibility standards, migration assumptions, failure paths, and conditions for reopening old choices. It allows a new model or developer to understand why the system is shaped as it is. It also lets the team revise those reasons when conditions change.

In a research archive, the layer contains claim status, evidence changes, category failures, summary cautions, unresolved tensions, and standards for closure. It helps the inquiry remain continuous without pretending that old uncertainty is always current uncertainty.

These layers may look different in practice. The form is less important than the function. The layer preserves the work's return structure in a way that can be read, corrected, and moved.

The same structure can apply beyond the three recurring cases. A product organization may preserve the reasoning behind a strategic thesis. A public institution may preserve why a policy threshold was set. A design team may preserve the conditions under which one user group was prioritized over another. In each case, the layer is valuable only if later humans can inspect and revise it.

The broader point is not that every field needs the same format. The layer will look different in different domains. What must remain constant is the boundary: retained context should support re-entry, not decide what re-entry means.

13.6 What the Layer Must Resist

The layer must resist opacity. If the user cannot see what memory contains, memory becomes authority by hidden inheritance.

It must resist captivity. If the user cannot move the layer, continuity becomes enclosure.

It must resist completeness as a false ideal. A total record is not the same as a useful continuity structure. Too much undifferentiated memory can bury judgment.

It must resist doctrine. If prior decisions cannot be reopened, the layer becomes a machine for preserving stale judgment.

It must resist model ownership. A model may operate on the layer, but it should not own the layer, decide what the layer means, or determine which history deserves authority.

These resistances are maintenance practices, not final guarantees. The layer can decay, carry old errors, preserve refusals past their usefulness, and make a project too loyal to its former self. That is why the human must retain the power to delete inherited context, revise old standards, reopen settled questions, and refuse fluent continuity.

13.7 The Final Boundary

The cognitive layer does not promise safety. It does not solve judgment. It does not remove dependence on tools, models, archives, institutions, or other people. It names the structure needed when cognition has already begun to extend outward.

The book began with a person returning to a project and discovering that the files were not enough. It moved through remembered tools, continuity, cognitive presence, persistent collaboration, memory's illusion, externalized cognition, archives, project recognition, cognitive loss, portability, judgment authority, and agency.

The pressure remained consistent. What helps return can also enclose. What remembers can also mislead. What preserves continuity can also harden into authority. Externalized cognition can support human judgment, but judgment cannot be outsourced.

This final boundary should remain restrained. Not a human replaced by intelligence. Not a machine that knows the person. Not a platform that owns memory. A human works through externalized cognition while remaining answerable for judgment.

The cognitive layer is therefore not the triumph of external memory. It is a way to keep external memory subordinate to human responsibility. It allows work to survive interruption without pretending that survival is authority. It allows models to assist without allowing inference to become judgment. It allows history to travel without requiring the present to obey it.

The book ends here because the remaining task is not another concept. It is maintenance. The layer has to be kept legible. The model has to be kept in its place. The human has to keep the burden of judgment, even when the surrounding system makes acceptance easier.

The lasting object is not the model.

The model performs inference.

The layer carries partial continuity.

The human remains answerable for judgment.

That is the cognitive layer: not an escape from fragility, but a way of keeping fragility visible enough to judge.

Boundary

The layer supports return.

It does not govern the human.

Appendix: A Minimal Cognitive Layer Record

A cognitive layer does not need to preserve everything. It should preserve enough of the project's return structure for a future human, team, or system to re-enter the work responsibly.

Current Orientation

What is the project trying to do now? What is the live question? What has changed since earlier decisions were made?

Active Decisions

Which decisions are still shaping the work? Which decisions are historical but no longer active?

Decision Conditions

Under what conditions was each important decision responsible? What would require reconsideration?

Refusal List

Which paths were considered and rejected? Were they rejected as principles, or only under specific circumstances?

Unresolved Tensions

Which questions should remain open? Which tensions must not be flattened into premature conclusions?

Working Standards

What standards currently govern the work: tone, reversibility, evidentiary caution, naming discipline, interpretive restraint, or other project-specific constraints?

Failure Memory

Which attempts failed in a way the project should not have to rediscover? What did each failure teach?

Stale Assumptions

Which inherited assumptions may no longer hold? Which old constraints might now be misleading?

Ownership Notes

Who owns the decision? Who can revise the record? Where does consequence land?

This record is not an authority over the work. It is a structure for return. It should remain readable, revisable, portable, and subordinate to human judgment.

About the Author

Xiaoqing Wang is a systems-focused engineer and technical writer interested in judgment, tools, institutional memory, and the practical consequences of software-mediated work.

His work examines how externalized cognition changes attention, memory, responsibility, and human agency in long-running projects.

www.ingramcontent.com/pod-product-compliance
Lightning Source LLC
LaVergne TN
LVHW100323210926
848480LV00003B/1242